MY FATHER GAVE ME A SERPENT

My Father Gave Me a Serpent

PATRICIA ZIMMERMAN

Published by
chosen books
FLEMING H. REVELL COMPANY
OLD TAPPAN, NEW JERSEY

Library of Congress Cataloging in Publication Data

Zimmerman, Patricia.
My father gave me a serpent.

1. Zimmerman, Patricia. 2. Converts—United States—Biography. 3. Alcoholics—United States—Biography. 4. Strahlendorff, Arthur. I. Title.
BV4935.Z56A35 1985 280'.4 [B] 85-26353
ISBN 0-8007-9054-5

Edited by David Hazard
and Ann McMath
Designed by Ann Cherryman

A Chosen Book

Chosen Books are Published by
Fleming H. Revell Company
Old Tappan, New Jersey
Printed in the United States of America

For my grandson,
Nathan

Acknowledgments

My deepest gratitude goes out to my very dear friends, Helen Pottinger, Elizabeth Schoene, Anne Santi, Meg Stimson, Marie Coen, and all of the people at St. Paul's Parish, Brookfield, Connecticut, whose continued encouragement and faithful prayers gave me so much strength while writing this book.

A very special thank you to Juliet Fay, who so patiently typed the manuscript.

And my heartfelt thanks to David Hazard and Ann McMath, editors at Chosen Books, whose sensitive guidance and supportive skill helped to make this book a reality.

Prologue

A phone was ringing, rousing me from a troubled sleep. Drowsily, I picked up the receiver on my bedside table and glanced at the clock. Six-fifteen. My head felt fuzzy. "Hello?" I mumbled into the receiver.

The dial tone hummed in my ear. I hung up, sat on the edge of the bed and shook myself awake.

It was the dream again. For days I had evaded the silent reproach of that telephone, and for several nights in a row it had invaded my sleep. I couldn't put it off any longer. Today I had to call the nursing home.

By 7:30 I had dressed, fed the children, Chris and Jennifer, and ushered them out to the school bus. The house was suddenly quiet. I lingered over my second cup of coffee.

I had been feeling cramped in our small kitchen. It had been a big adjustment from the spacious house overlooking the lake our family had lived near for eight years. I wondered if I'd ever get used to all the changes in my life, now that I was single again. A single parent, others might say I was "liberated." I laughed to myself. Liberated for what? Anxieties, fears, guilt, bills I couldn't pay? If only our marriage hadn't gotten so bad, if only I could have found a way sooner, if only . . .

"Stop it!" I said out loud. "Today is the first day of the rest of my life." I announced the glib proclamation with a conviction I couldn't feel. There is no use rummaging through a past I can't change. I can't wallow in a swamp of "If only's." I have to live *today*. *In* today.

So why should I make this phone call, I wondered? Isn't that dredging up even deeper hurts? Why should I reach out to that man, and open up old emotional wounds? Why should I sort out all that wreckage from my childhood? I didn't cause it, I didn't. . . .

That's enough, I ordered my racing mind. *You can't squirm off this hook, my girl. You know the right thing to do. And you can't control the results. Trust God. Remember? He has a plan for your life.*

Yes, I had to believe that. And this phone call was part of the plan. Would I ever relinquish my will, once and for all? Could God bring some true good out of years of hurt?

Well, I thought, *Now, I have to get on with it!*

I walked into the bedroom and sat down by the phone. The number was there on the message pad where I had written it three days before.

"Sunny Acres Nursing Home, good morning." The voice was briskly cheerful.

"Hello. This is Mrs. Zimmerman. I'm calling about one of your patients."

"Yes, Mrs. Zimmerman. This is Mrs. Burns, the nursing supervisor. How can I help you?"

I gave her his name.

"Yes, he's with us," she responded.

"I just learned a few days ago that he has been quite ill."

"Oh, yes. He's had two strokes and his condition is very serious. He hasn't been able to take food for several days, and I'm afraid he's failing rapidly. Have you been out to visit him here?"

"No, I haven't. I didn't know—where he was. I spoke with my aunt last week and she told me he'd been taken to your nursing home."

"That's right. He was doing well the first week he came here from the hospital. But, as you know, his age is a factor. The recuperative powers aren't what they used to be. Did you see him when he was in the hospital?"

I hesitated. This was all so awkward.

"No," I said. "I haven't seen him for—quite a while."

"Are you a relative, Mrs. Zimmerman?"

"Yes," I said. "I am. I'm his daughter."

She paused a moment. Perhaps she, too, felt the awkwardness. "Oh, I see. I didn't know he had a daughter."

"Mrs. Burns," I said, "I want to see my father. Could I come out to the nursing home?"

She hesitated, "He's hardly conscious now, and we don't expect his condition to change for the better. I wish I could be more hopeful, but there really isn't much time left for him. Do come. As soon as possible."

I took a deep breath. "I'll come tomorrow. Would you give me directions? I'll be driving from Connecticut."

I carefully took down her instructions, thanked her, and told her I would be there in the morning.

I hung up the phone and lay back on the bed, my eyes closed. I felt totally exhausted.

Did you see your father when he was in the hospital? No, Mrs. Burns, I haven't seen him for—a while. I haven't seen my father for sixteen years.

MY FATHER GAVE ME A SERPENT

Chapter One

My father was a large man, with piercing eyes, powerful hands, and a thundering voice that filled the house of my childhood.

And I knew he'd be home any minute.

Barely tall enough to see over the window sill at the top of the stairs, I waited, as I did each evening at six o'clock. On tiptoe at my lookout post, I watched for the first glimpse of his car turning into the driveway. My heart drummed with anticipation, somewhere between hope and dread. Would it be all right today?

My first grade spelling paper was clutched in my hand. An A plus! A pluses were very special. I hoped Daddy would think I was *very* special today.

I heard the sound of a car coming up the street. Was it his? I could hardly see the sun-dappled street through the heavy shade trees. Yes, there it was, a black car with a dent in the fender. The car slowed and turned into our driveway at 309 Warwick Avenue.

Daddy was home! I plunged down the stairs, then stopped halfway. In a moment the kitchen door slammed. Mother was already home from teaching at the university. I waited to hear their voices. I could barely pick up the words they were saying to each other, but when I heard my mother's laugh I knew it was safe.

"Oh, Arthur, what a thing to say!" Mother's voice filtered up the stairway, responsive and happy. My father's hearty laughter joined in. The sound drew me irresistibly down the stairs and into the bright kitchen.

"Hello there, Little One, how's my best girl?"

My father leaned down and kissed me on the forehead, then lifted me in his strong arms high above him to touch the ceiling. He grinned up at me and my heart flooded with joy. At those happy times I loved his wide smile, the twinkling gray eyes behind the steel-rimmed glasses, the fine, light hair that barely covered his pale scalp. As he lowered me to him, I thrust my spelling paper in front of his face and whispered in his ear, "Daddy, I got an A plus today."

"You did? You got an A plus? Well, that deserves a special prize. What will it be, Little One? You just name it."

"Oh, Daddy, can I really?"

"Why, sure you can, you just name it!" he said, lowering me to the floor. Maybe he would take me with him Sunday, when he went fishing. He always went in the early morning, when nobody else was awake. Could I dare ask? Trembling, I took a deep breath.

"Daddy—" I could barely whisper, "Could I—could we—"

But now he was by the stove talking to Mother as she briskly stirred the gravy. "Anita, that jerk I work for has to give me another car! I'm supposed to sell his new 1935 models and I'm driving around in a junk heap. The worst lemon on the lot. I told that bum there was something wrong with the carburetor, but, no, he wouldn't listen to me."

My mother nodded sympathetically as she spooned out the home fries on our dinner plates. She handed me my plate and said, "Go sit down, Patty."

I tugged my father's sleeve. "Daddy, can we—my prize—can we—" He brushed my hand away.

"You heard your mother, Patty, now sit down and eat." His warm tone was gone. I sat down at the table.

"Can we—later—" I began again.

"Not now!" He commanded loudly. "It's time to eat."

"Later?" I whispered.

But he had forgotten already. *Maybe,* I thought, *I can try again, later.* It was so hard to know how and when to speak so he would hear me. *When I'm bigger, I'll know how,* I promised myself. *I'll get more A pluses and I'll know how to say the words and he'll say yes.* Despondently, I poked at the home fries with my fork.

But, more often, were the bad times. Many times I cringed on the stairs at six o'clock, afraid to go down into the storms of anger. On those nights I would run to the shelter of my room, close the door and wait on the edge of my bed. In a while the door would open quietly and my brother, Edward, would come in and sit down. Ed was three years older, and bigger, and he knew more about the storms. Sometimes he would tell me what made them happen. I didn't always understand, but it didn't matter, as long as *I* didn't make them happen.

There were a lot of Other Things that brought the storms, Ed explained to me. There were money things, and work things, and church things, and

Mother's family. After Grandma moved in with us, she was one of the Other Things. I couldn't understand how Grandma, who loved us so much, could make the storms happen, but Ed assured me it was so.

One night, the shouting voices jarred me from sleep. I shivered under my blankets, and waited. Soon, the door opened and Ed slipped into the room. "They're awful loud tonight," he said, slumping on the edge of the bed.

"What's wrong this time, Ed?" I asked him. He looked very wise and grown up, even in his rumpled pajamas with his brown hair tousled from sleep.

"It's money," he said solemnly.

"What money?" I thought of the green papers in my mother's black handbag.

"It's not the money that's *here,* Patty." In the dim light, his thin shoulders seemed to shake. So did his voice. "It's the money that *isn't* here."

"Where is it? Did somebody lose it?"

"No, I don't think so." He paused a moment. A frown creased his forehead. "I think it's the money they can't get."

I was puzzled. "Why can't they get it, Ed? Why don't they buy some?"

"You can't buy money, Patty, you have to get it. From work." He was right, I didn't understand.

"But Daddy works. And so does Mama. I know *that!* So why don't they get money?"

"I can't explain it, Patty, I'm too tired and it's too—complicated!" He pulled himself up and patted my arm. "Go to sleep. At least it isn't us this time."

He slipped quietly out the door and I lay very still in the dark, waiting for quiet to come.

Those were not the worst nights. There were others—ugly, ragged nights, when the storm would gather suddenly and ravage my haven of sleep. . . .

I was swimming in a warm, sparkling pool, diving down to the white sandy bottom where fluted sea shells glowed with bright jewels, red and green and blue, and there were glittering fish swimming all around me. I reached out to touch them. I was gliding and breathing in the water, just like the fish. A shining pearl lay on the white sand just below me. It glowed with a hazy pink light. How lovely it was, and it was for me, my pearl. I dove down to pick it up. . . . A shrill scream pierced the water—the fish were suddenly huge and black and their teeth were tearing at my legs, stinging me. . . . "Oh, stop, please stop!" I screamed, and the pond was gone and the pearl was gone and the stinging leather of my father's strap thrashed across my writhing body.

"I'll teach you, you good-for-nothing—"

"Stop! Daddy, please stop!" I tried to shield my legs, but the belt bit at my arms and hands.

"Say you're sorry!" he shouted.

"I'm sorry, I'm sorry, I'm sorry!" I screamed, near hysteria. I didn't know what I was sorry for, but it didn't matter, if only he would stop. When I couldn't breathe through my choking sobs, when I couldn't endure another moment, the lashing suddenly stopped.

"You'll do what you're told, or next time I'll give you a licking you'll never forget!" The light went out, the door slammed. He was gone. I wept into my pillow, holding my aching legs. Soon that pain dulled, but the helpless rage consuming me burned in my heart far into the night.

Some nights I'd wake to Ed's cries. I'd pull the pillow over my head to shut them out, thankful they weren't mine—and guilty, for being glad they weren't.

The night storms struck Mother, too. Blurred shouting broke the silence. Heavy footsteps shook the stairs. Doors slammed shut. An engine started, and my father's car tore into the night. In the darkness, my mother wept.

On Sundays, we went to church—Grandma, Ed and I. Sometimes Mother went too. Never my father.

I knew church was about God, who made everything. There was music, and a man in a long robe stood in front with his hands stretched out while we knelt down. He said words about God, but I didn't understand them. The air had a strange, sweet smell. Church took a long time, and my knees hurt a lot.

God was chiefly about being good. I wondered if church could make me good. It didn't make Ed good. Grandma was good already.

My father said he didn't like church. He didn't seem to worry about being good. I wondered if God was one of the Other Things that caused the storms.

Sometimes there were party nights, evening when the downstairs rooms echoed with music, clinking glasses, and choruses of laughter. I loved the party nights. Our furnishings were comfortable, not lavish, but Mother saw to it that everything looked neat and in place. Ed and I, wrapped in our night robes, heads still damp from the bath, sat at the top of the stairs, waiting for Mother to call up to us.

While Ed hung back, I rushed into the room of happy grownups, who hugged me and ruffled my hair. Sometimes, they said nice, attentive things like, "Oh, she's adorable, Anita. She has your blue eyes," or, "How big you're getting, Patty, and prettier all the time." They fed me morsels of party food and let me sip the punch. I loved the way everything smelled; the food, the perfume, the pipes and cigarettes—the wine. My father would smile at me approvingly, then send me off to bed, to lie awake in the dark, listening to the grownups laughing as my father amused them with one of his famous fishing adventures.

In the morning when I went downstairs, the empty room was cold and disheveled. There were plates of half-finished food on the table, and glasses littered about. Once I tasted the amber liquid in a half-empty glass. It was stale and bitter.

My parents slept late after party nights and were sullen when they came downstairs. Ed and I had to be very quiet. They were uncertain hours. A storm could break at any time.

When I was seven, I made my First Communion. In a white dress, white veil, and white shoes, I knelt at the altar and received the flat, tasteless wafer, trembling with joy. I knew that now I would know how to be good. I knew that God would be pleased, and the storms wouldn't come anymore.

My father didn't come to church to see my First Communion. I heard him tell Mother that it was a lot of nonsense. But he said I was pretty in my white dress.

Later that year, Grandmother died. I missed her terribly, her loving acceptance, her constant warmth. My mother continued to take Ed and me to church to receive Communion, because her mother would have wanted her to. She waited outside in the car until church was over.

I liked to receive Communion, but somehow it was disappointing. It didn't make me good enough to stop the storms.

On Saturday nights Ed and I went to confession. I knelt in the dark cubicle and timidly whispered my sins to a shadowy form behind a grill. Then I went to the altar to say my penance. I looked up at the image of Jesus, nailed to the cross, the drained face, the bleeding side, the thorns pressed into the skull. It disturbed me, and I vowed I would sin no more. His father sent him to die on the cross, Sister Theresa had said, to save us.

I wasn't sure I trusted His father, a father who would not save his son.

Even so, each Sunday I took the pale wafer on my tongue and hoped it would do its miraculous work on my tarnished soul.

In June, as soon as Mother's school year ended, we went to the river cabin. It was small, with bare floors, exposed rafters, a woodstove, kerosene lamps and a hand pump in the sink. Tucked into the woods looking over the Delaware Valley, it was my paradise. We roamed through the woods, Ed, Cousin Tommy, and I, swam, climbed, built fortresses, and crowned ourselves rulers of this kingdom where every good thing would always happen.

My father came up on weekends. He loved to go out on the river alone even before sunrise and fish for timeless hours. Afternoons he piled us into the car and drove us through the mountains he loved so well. Later, he took us to the village store and bought ice cream cones. In the evenings, he built a charcoal fire and we feasted on the catch of the day, rainbow trout and speckled bass. And there was roasted corn, juicy red tomatoes, and fresh milk. It was all nectar.

On the days when it was too chilly to swim, I loved to walk down the winding road past our cabin and climb the hill to an old cemetery hidden from view by trees and underbrush. I wandered through the gravestones and read the weathered inscriptions. I sat down on a fallen stone and thought about God and Grandma and all those people under the ground who were in heaven now. I wondered how God could know all of His children by their first names, and love all of them at the same time.

The summer I was eight, I awaited the vacation journey with a fierce excitement. My father had finally promised to take me fishing with him. The night before we left I could hardly sleep. How wonderful it would be, just the two of us out on the river! I would catch the biggest fish and he would be so proud of me. He'd tell all his friends, and he'd take me fishing all the time.

In the morning the sky was gray and heavy. We drove to the river valley through torrents of pouring rain. I prayed it would clear by the time we arrived, but the deluge continued. We returned to the cabin and waited through the day and all through the next three days and nights. Listlessly, Ed and Tommy and I played cards at the kitchen table by the woodstove and read our dog-eared collection of comic books by lamplight. Every hour I went out on the porch and searched the heavens for a patch of blue sky. Down below the cabin the swollen brown river rushed by, sweeping logs and branches along in its thundering rapids. I had never seen the river like that.

"Daddy, when will it stop?"

My father was on the porch arranging weights and hooks and dry flies in his gear box.

"I don't know, Little One. Looks like this week's a washout for me. I've got to go to work tomorrow."

My heart sank. "Oh, Daddy, when will we go fishing?"

"Not until this rain lets up, I'm afraid."

I fought back the tears. He looked over at me, and said, "I'll tell you what, Little One. As soon as the rain lets up, you and Ed and Tommy can go fishing."

"But I want to got with *you,* " I pleaded.

He studied his gear box for a moment. "Patty, bring your fishing rod over here. I've got something special for you."

My fishing pole was in the corner at the far end of the porch. I brought it over to him. He picked out a brightly colored fishing fly from the box, along with a sinker and a hook. Carefully he attached them to my fishing line.

"Now, Patty, this is my very best trout fly. I tied it myself, and I've caught more fish with it than any other fly I've ever used."

"It's beautiful, Daddy." Above the barb, it looked like a silky miniature rainbow.

"When the river calms down the three of you can go fishing right out here where the water is shallow and you can walk across to the sandbar. And next weekend, you can show me all the fish you caught."

Somehow this little bit of special attention solved my disappointment. He showed me how to cast the line, letting it soar through the air high over the ground, and how to reel it back. It was thrilling to watch him.

"You be very careful with this fly, Patty. Remember, it's the very best I have. Don't you lose it!"

"I'll be careful, Daddy, I promise. I felt a solemn sort of joy at the tremendous honor he had bestowed upon me. I felt very grown-up and proud that he trusted me with his valuable treasure.

The rain continued through the next morning and slowed to a drizzle by late afternoon. That evening we could see stars in the sky and we knew it would clear the next day. In the morning we went down to the river. The water was still an ugly brown, still a swift-moving current. Discouraged, we went back to the cabin to wait.

Two days later, the river seemed clearer and

calmer. Mother was resistant, but we pestered until she relented and said we could go.

"Be careful, and stay in front of the house where I can see you," she cautioned.

"We'll just wade out to the sandbar, Mom. We'll be careful," I promised.

Wearing my fishing hat, bathing suit and sneakers, and proudly carrying my rod with its hand-tied treasure, I trailed Ed and Tommy down to the river. They waded in first and I followed. But as I tried to move forward, the current pushed against me. Ed and Tommy were far ahead, halfway to the sandbar. What was happening? At once the water, which was usually no higher than my waist, was up to my chest, and my feet were slipping. I gripped my pole in both hands and raised it over my head. I called out to Ed, but he didn't hear me. He and Tommy were already on the sandbar. Suddenly, the river was washing me downstream.

Helpless, like a fallen branch, I was swept toward the rapids, where the water slapped against the rocks.

Oh, God, I prayed, struggling futilely, *please don't let me lose my fishing pole.*

The churning waters pounded about my face, and I could see the white rapids breaking over the jagged rocks. "God, help me, please help me!" I sputtered. In a split second of time, I knew I had to free my hands to swim—to let go of the pole, or be dashed on the rocks.

I kicked off my sneakers, took a deep breath, and let go of the pole. The current pressed against me, but I thrashed my arms and legs, fighting it, my lungs bursting for air, praying frantically. *God, please get me to the other side—please keep me up—*

In only moments, I was spent. My limbs could

hardly move. I couldn't fight any longer. Too exhausted to struggle, my leaden legs sank.

To my relief, my feet touched bottom. I could stand. I had made it! Gasping for breath, I pulled myself up on the shore, out of the dark water. Ed and Tommy were running down the sandbar toward me.

"What did you do? Why didn't you follow us?" Ed sounded angry.

"I couldn't, Ed, the water was too deep. It pushed me. And—and—" I burst into tears, "I dropped my fishing pole!"

"That's okay, Patty," said Tommy, and he put his arm around me.

"Oh, no, no it isn't. I lost Daddy's best fishing fly."

When my father arrived late the following night, I hid in my room. I heard him in the kitchen talking to Mother and pulled the covers over my head. In a moment, the door opened and Father was standing by my bed.

"Daddy, I'm sorry, I didn't mean to . . . I couldn't help it, I couldn't swim with the pole, the water was . . ."

He sat on my bed, then pulled me into his arms. "Well, Little One," he said gently, "don't you worry about it." He stroked my head.

"But your best fishing fly . . ."

"You know," he said softly, gently rocking me, "I think I'd rather have my best girl than any old fishing fly."

My heart soared. My body flooded with the warmth of his soothing embrace. I didn't care if I ever went fishing again. I had everything I wanted. he loved me. He really loved me!

In years to come, I would remember this hallowed time when I knew beyond question that my father loved me. And over the years to come, in my dreams, I would swim upstream through that endless dark river, searching for a lost cabin hidden on a distant shore.

Chapter Two

Those summers were golden times: carefree days of play, gentle starlit evenings, and peaceful nights. I prayed they would never end.

But each year, all too soon, it was time to leave. Ed and I returned to our grammar school, and my mother to her French classes.

Ed and I learned slowly, painfully, as the storms continued, how to find our way through them. We learned to pick up early warning signals, to dodge, evade, and to simulate a calm we didn't feel. We learned when to team up, and when to go it alone.

Ed grew into a quiet, awkward boy, studious and painfully shy. And I became a dreamer.

On cold winter mornings, I'd awaken to the urgent clattering of my mother's heels hurrying down the stairs in her usual rush to get breakfast and drive off to school. I burrowed into my blankets, postponing the dreaded moment when I had to gather up my clothes and huddle over the hall radiator to dress. I'd spin a waking dream of a warm house, and a closet bursting with gorgeous dresses. The fantasies continued through the day.

Trudging to school, through rain-drenched leaves

in autumn, ankle-deep snow in winter, I had only to open the gates of imagination and a golden palomino would appear, mane lashing in the wind, to carry me away. We left the sullen streets behind. Even though I enjoyed school, any tedious moments could be transformed by dream trips to Wonderland, Oz, Shangri-La, and Hollywood. Whenever I wanted to escape, a custom-designed fantasy was ready to take me away.

And at night, lying in the dark, the terror of my parents' battles was stilled by the waking dreams that became ever more vivid and extravagant. I was the living heroine of every book I read, every movie I saw. No matter that I was small and skinny and couldn't keep my shoe laced tied. In a moment I adorned myself with a lissome body, flowing tresses, and danced down an alabaster staircase with Fred Astaire in quick pursuit. I was as bold as Barbara Stanwyck, graceful as Ginger Rogers, poised as Greer Garson, and triumphant in all situations. In those childhood days, I wore my private world like an invisible cloak for warmth and shelter against the bitter seasons of reality.

My brother and I became wiser about our parent's struggle. We couldn't fathom the cause of the war, but we learned the logistics of the battles. We knew when the battle was about money or my father's rage against the church, when it was about relatives or friends or something she had said or something he had said. I came to understand that, even though I lived on a quiet, sun-dappled street lined with comfortable homes, there were dangers lurking everywhere. Things were not as they seemed.

The church was especially dangerous. It was full of hypocrites, my father said. On Sunday mornings I furtively searched the faces around me, trying to recognize the hypocrites. There was Mrs. Nelson who lived on our block, sweet, demure, softspoken. Was she one of them? And Mr. Kemper, who came every Sunday with his wife and four children. He seemed so kind and friendly. Could he be one of the "two-faced phonies"? It was troubling. I didn't know what a hypocrite looked like. When the priest spoke solemnly about loving our neighbors I wondered how that was possible, if the people who seemed so good and loving were really evil at heart. I couldn't unravel this mystery, and hoped that when I grew up, I would understand these things.

I had looked forward to the party all day. It wasn't as exciting as it had been when I was younger, but I enjoyed helping Mother polish the silver, and prepare the food. I was glad the house would soon be filled with people, laughing and relaxing over their drinks.

My mother looked pretty that night, with her dark hair combed back into its usual modest coil. Her fair, oval face glowed with excitement and a touch of rouge. She was wearing her prettiest dress, the navy gabardine with the wide collar that flattered her slight figure. She wore no jewelry but dabbed the barest trace of Lily of the Valley behind her ears.

My father was downstairs in his darkroom, selecting special prints to show the guests. His interest in photography had started out as a casual hobby, but turned into a new career. He was gifted, and people throughout the area were eager to sit for his sensitive portraits. I was very proud of his beautiful pictures, bedecked with prize ribbons from the many competitions he entered. He had built the darkroom himself and installed the best equipment money could buy. His confidence seemed to expand with the recognition. So, with Mother's salary to sustain us, he ventured into a future bright with possibility.

My father came upstairs with his collection of prints at the first ring of the doorbell. That was the time I loved the best.

"Can I answer it, Daddy?"

He put the prints on the dining room table. "Okay, Patty, you can be the welcoming committee."

I felt like a grown-up hostess, greeting the guests and taking their coats into the spare bedroom.

The Shermans were the first to arrive, along with the Mayers. Mrs. Mayer and Mrs. Sherman were sisters, my mother's friends. Their husbands had fished and hunted with my father for many years.

"Well, Patty," said one neighbor woman, hugging me, "what a pretty dress." It was so good to be a part of a party night.

Next came the Dowds. Mr. Dowd was an avid fisherman. He and my father had waded through every trout stream in the northeast. Then Mr. Harkins, who was also an avid photographer. In one arm was his own portfolio, and on the other arm, his tiny, birdlike wife.

"Come on in here, folks!" My father called from the living room. "Drinks are on the house." While my father took charge of the gathering, I took the last of the coats upstairs.

The doorbell rang as I was coming back down. My father went to the door.

"Well, its about time you got here!" My father's oldest friends, the Farmers, had arrived.

They came into the hall with a woman I had never seen before. She was ushered into the living room for introductions.

"Pay attention, everyone!" said Mrs. Farmer. I want you to meet Clara Watson." The request was unnecessary, for Clara Watson commanded attention. Sweeping into the room in a cloud of shimmering blue chiffon, she tossed her mink stole on the sofa. She was a tall, fleshy woman with billowing red hair. Rings glittered on her fingers and gold bracelets jangled as she moved. The scent of her musky perfume reached me where I had paused on the stairs.

"Greetings, gang!" she announced in a deep throaty voice. She turned to my father. "I'll take a scotch on the rocks with a lemon twist, kind sir, and the best seat in the house!" Her husky laugh captured her audience as she sprawled into a wide armchair.

"Wow! That's a load off my feet!" Stretching out her long legs, she shook off her spike-heeled, silver sandals and let them drop to the floor. "You're looking at sixty dollars' worth of torture chambers. I swear, I gotta see a shrink—or a foot doctor! I don't know which should come first!" She threw her head back and laughed again.

All eyes were riveted on her, and soon, the men had eased into her careless banter, offering to massage her feet, or carry her to the sofa. Her voice and laughter suffused the room with a restless energy. The party tempo quickened. Glasses emptied rapidly and were quickly filled again. Everyone was talking and laughing at once. Someone put a record on the phonograph.

"Come on, Clara," one man challenged. "Let's give those feet a workout."

Clara stood up, clapped her hands over her head, and sauntered across the room in her stockinged feet, and they began to dance. Others paired off, and soon they were caught up in a whirling fever of gaiety. A rising chorus of saxophones blared through the house.

It wasn't like any other party night. I felt awkward, out of place. I could see they wouldn't be interested in looking at pictures. Unnoticed, I slipped upstairs to my room, relieved to escape the frantic mood that had overtaken the evening. I felt uneasy. Everything was different about this party and I knew that the reason was Clara.

My parents responded to Clara in a way they had never before responded to anyone. She was totally different from my parents' circle of friends, and her difference set her apart, like a hybrid orchid in a field of daisies. They seemed starved for the diversion she offered and loved her reckless excitement. Within a few months Clara had slowly worked her way into our family's daily routine, as if she were not an outsider but a supporting pillar.

They now spent long evenings making plans, with Clara as a constant contributor and sounding board. They began going out, the three of them, to dinner, clubs, shows, weekend photography trips, always together. Clara never failed to arrive with a bottle of scotch, and long before the evening was over, the bottle was always empty. My parents began to put in their own supply. Mother drank very little, but my father and Clara seemed to have an endless thirst and a limitless capacity.

I had conflicting feelings about Clara. Part of me vicariously enjoyed the excitement, but part of me resented her intrusion. And besides the change in our family, I was changing. My adolescent moods swung up and down often pitching me into turmoil. Life was changing inside of me and all around me as well.

One change was truly remarkable. My parents had stopped quarreling. It seemed to me they were suddenly filled with heady excitement, fueled by a constant flow of alcohol. An unplanned truce formed between them. The truce held until the time when Clara went away for two weeks, during which they fought. When she reappeared, the white flag went up. I found I was relieved to have her back. If peace could come, even through an intruder, I welcomed it.

That year I entered high school. The new environment was a rude shock. I realized how much of a haven my grammar school had been. I felt thrust into a huge building crowded with teenagers who were far more sophisticated than I. My face erupted with ugly blotches and suddenly, I had a weight problem. Girls I had known since kindergarten were no longer my friends. They clustered together in the hallways exchanging gossip breathlessly about who was dating, who was breaking up, what clothes were right, and how everyone ranked on the popularity scale.

I was lost and without one close friend.

I desperately longed to go back to the childhood that had vanished so abruptly. At home I was more alone than ever. Ed was preparing for graduation. In September he would go to college. He had been accepted at my mother's alma mater, a prestigious ivy league school. Because of the cost there was never talk of my going to college and I wondered what my future would be.

Too backward socially to date or go to dances and parties, I took up baby sitting, and spent my weekends in other people's homes. I read stories to children of all ages, and created my own serial adventures to entertain them. I poured out all the frustrated love I had to give, and they received it eagerly. A failure with my peers, I became the most popular sitter in the neighborhood.

My school work was erratic. I couldn't concentrate and I had no confidence in myself to learn any new subjects. I gave up easily, unless I was sure of my competence. And I continued to daydream, but now the dreams were of escape into a future where I would be successful, attractive, popular with boys, envied by girls, and able to accomplish any goal to which I aspired. I longed now for achievable dreams in the real world.

The next summer, when we went to the river, Clara went too. I had the same room at the front of the cabin with a window facing the porch. The woods seemed as cool and tranquil as before, the river valley as peaceful, but everything was different. Ed had gone away with friends for two weeks. My father didn't go out early in the morning to fish. He and mother and Clara now went out to the local night spots, or sat together on the porch, drinking late into the night. She dominated even my parents' social life. They saw almost no one else but her. After a week I couldn't wait to go back home. I had never felt that way before. Clara had invaded my private paradise.

One night a few days before we were to leave, I was awakened by the sound of voices coming from the porch. Clara was crying—harsh racking sobs. She sounded drunk.

"What is there for me?" she wailed. "What kind of life can I have, a woman alone? Oh, you two can't understand. What do you know about being lonely? After all those years, taking care of an invalid, and then he dies, leaving me so alone."

"Clara, you know he loved you very much. . . ." My mother was trying to comfort her, but the effort only brought a fresh outburst of tears and slurred words.

"Oh, sure, you think I have it easy 'cause I have money, and a nice house, and lots of clothes, but I don't have anything. Nothing. Sometimes I think—" She paused a moment, and I heard the ice clinking in her glass. "Sometimes I think I'll just end it all. That's the best thing." She was sobbing heavily again. "No good. No good for anything."

"Don't say that, Clara," my father said abruptly. "Here, have another drink. You'll feel better."

"I just want to sleep . . . never wake up. . . ."

"We'd better get her to bed, Arthur. I think she's passed out."

I heard them lift her from her chair and lead her through the kitchen into the spare room.

I was frightened. I wished Clara would go away, and never come back. I wanted to talk to someone, but there was no one to listen. I was alone with my fear.

In September we drove Ed to the university. Clara, of course, went with us. There was so much unspoken anguish in my heart that week, I found it impossible to talk to anyone. And then the house was so empty when we returned. I wanted to cry, but no tears came. And so began a pattern: My emotions billowed inside me, but, with no one to talk to, I buried them deep within.

Autumn of 1945 began a season of chaos. My parents and Clara entered a new phase of their relationship. My father's business venture in photography wasn't going well. My mother sold stock that Grandmother had left her in order to keep Edward in school and was resentful about it. They fought bitterly. Clara moved to the center of the conflicts. The evenings they spent together, drinks in hand, were now punctuated with sudden flares of angry words that continued long after Clara went home.

I became the focus of long lectures in the kitchen that dwelt mostly on my poor performance at school, my bad disposition, and the certainty that I would never amount to anything.

I dreaded bringing report cards home that fall. On my first one were two C's. The science grade was bad enough, but a C in French was my undoing.

As I expected, a long, grueling session took place in the kitchen that night. My father sat on the kitchen chair, drinking his beer, my mother hovered over the ironing board, and I stood silent before them.

"How could you disgrace me this way?" Mother began, her face tight with anger. "What will your teachers think of me? You, the daughter of a French teacher coming with a grade like that." She picked up the iron and furiously attacked a limp sleeve.

"You're not getting away with this, young lady," my father announced. He settled back in his chair and poured another glass of beer. "You're going to learn to work, the *hard* way. You'll come home right after school every day and study. And right after supper, you'll go back and study some more until bedtime. No movies on the weekends, no friends, no visits. Just school work, until there's a change in those marks.

"I'm not raising a good-for-nothing!" His look of angry disgust cut me deeper than the words.

I wanted to scream at them. I wanted to tell about the awful desolation I struggled with every day, to cry out, "Love me, please love me. Why don't you understand? I need to belong, I need—" The words were choked by the lump in my throat, words they would never hear.

One bright spot that winter was a playwriting contest at school. I entered and won first prize—an unexpected triumph. For a brief time my classmates noticed me. I brought home the school paper, which had an article about the contest, with my name in a headline.

"That's fine," said my father. "But I don't see that it makes any difference in the long run. Your grades are what count, and until we see some improvement there, don't expect any praise from us."

Would he never reward me—not with a single moment of togetherness—or a kind word? I put the article away in my desk drawer, and dreamed about winning a Pulitzer Prize.

In the spring I came down with the flu. I went to school one morning feeling chilled and feverish. By ten o'clock I was shaking all over. The school nurse examined me, and then promptly drove me home. The house was empty. I wearily climbed the stairs and crawled into bed, falling into a fevered sleep immediately.

It was afternoon when I woke to the sound of voices downstairs. Father was home—but why at this time of day? I got out of bed, to go tell him that I had been sent home. At the top of the stairs I stopped. I suddenly recognized the other voice. It was Clara's. I didn't move.

"I need to know what's going to happen to us, Arthur. You say you love me. Do you mean it?"

"Yes, Clara. You know I do." His voice was anxious, pleading.

"Then you have to leave her," Clara replied. "I

can't continue this way. We belong together. You know that."

Father spoke softly. "Just give me some time to work it out. I'll tell her soon."

"I want you, Arthur, more than anything in the world. You're my whole life."

"Yes, Clara. It'll be soon, very soon."

Shivering, I tiptoed into my room and carefully closed the door. I crept into bed. They hadn't heard me.

I was very ill for several weeks. The fever hung on, refusing to break. When at last it did, I was too sick to think about my father and Clara, too exhausted to comprehend what was happening to us. I shut it out of my mind, like a nightmare that had no reality.

That summer I was happily lifted out of the new storm that was gathering. I spent the warm, sunny months at the summer home of a neighbor family, helping take care of the children. But when I returned in the fall, the storm broke.

My parents were locked in combat. Onslaughts of ugly words burst through walls of cold silence.

Gradually, something inside of me was changing. Instead of pain, I felt a strange detachment, a high wall of indifference. In those cold months I learned to stop feeling, and I was grateful.

Ed didn't come home for Christmas that year. He was busy at school. I envied him his neutral ground.

The last battle was fought that winter. There were no winners.

One cold January night I was awakened by screaming. I huddled under the blanket terrified at the words that rose up from the living room.

"I'm through with you," my father roared.

"Oh, it's me is it?" my mother shrieked back at

him. "It's *my* fault—when you and that—that filth carry on together, right here in this house. You miserable excuse for a man. I've slaved for you, supported this family—"

"Oh, that's it again, isn't it? Not enough money for you—I'm not good enough for the high and mighty queen!" he roared back at her. "You and your smug family, for twenty years making me feel like a worm—"

My mother screamed. "You're no good, both of you, you and your filthy slut!"

"She's better than you've ever been. Better than you'll hope to be!"

"Then go to her, go, get out—I don't want you, I don't need you!"

Then, silence. It was over. I knew my father was leaving. He was leaving with Clara.

In the morning I sat alone at the kitchen table, watching an icy rain freeze on the windows. I heard his footsteps on the stairs. He came into the kitchen and stood behind my chair. Then he put his hand on the back of my head. I stared down at the empty plate in front of me.

"You're the only one I care about, Little One."

This is a great way to show it, I thought, guilty that he should say something loving to me when he hated my mother. I prayed she hadn't heard him.

He bent down and kissed me on the forehead. I didn't look up. His kiss made me feel like a traitor.

I heard his car pull out of the driveway and disappear into the rain.

Chapter Three

Mother wasn't home when I arrived from school at four o'clock. It was February, one month after Daddy left.

Before I took my coat off I ran down to the basement to stoke the coal furnace. I removed the ashes and shoveled fresh coal onto the burning embers. As I worked I kept my eyes from turning to the darkroom door a few feet away. My father's pictures and all of his equipment were still there, and I wondered if he would return for them. I wondered if he was living with Clara.

I went upstairs to the living room to wait for the heat to come up. It was deathly still. I wrapped myself in a blanket and curled up on the sofa while the house warmed. I sank into a daydream of sunny beaches and palm trees. But drifting off to sleep, I was again swimming upstream in the darkness . . . *the water was black and cold . . . I kept swimming, searching the shore line . . . there was a light far ahead, a single beacon shining out of the dark hillside . . . I swam on to reach it . . . the water seemed to hold me back, the current pushing against me . . . I had to reach the light . . . I had to keep moving up the dark river . . . a voice was calling me . . . Patty . . .*

"Patty, wake up." Mother was home. "Help me get the groceries out of the car."

I pulled myself up, and helped her lug the heavy packages into the kitchen.

"Did you tend the furnace, Patty? I hope you emptied the ashes. You know the fire can go out if you don't."

"I did it already, Mom." I didn't like to hear the anxiety that ran under my mother's questions.

It was also difficult for me to talk to her. I didn't know what to say to her. I could see the hurt in her eyes, hear the grief in her voice. I didn't want it to grip me. I wanted to stay within a safe, hidden place inside myself. I felt guilty about my detachment, but I couldn't change it. A numbing coldness had paralyzed my feelings. It was as though I had slipped into a coma, and the waking part of me was casually observing a twin imposter who had taken my place.

Mom went on talking. "I got some lamb chops. They were on sale this week. Are you hungry?"

"No, Mom. Not really." I hated sitting through the long silent meals. Even more, I hated the times when she talked about Daddy. I sat and picked at my lamb chops and, thankfully, Mother was silent.

After we'd finished with the dishes, Mother went upstairs to bed. I knew she would cry herself to sleep. It had become a ritual. I had tried to comfort her at first, but my efforts were fruitless. I was no help to her. She didn't seem to need me. *Edward will know how to handle it,* I thought. *Maybe she'll be better when he comes home from college.*

That evening, I had agreed to baby-sit for the Simpson children, who lived across the street. It was a welcome relief to be in other people's houses. We needed the money, but more important to me was the needed escape. When I returned home late at night the house would be dark and quiet. I wouldn't have to lie awake and listen to Mother grieving.

An icy wind had risen as the darkness settled in, so I wrapped up in my warmest clothes, pulled on my boots and called upstairs, "Mom, I'm going now."

For a moment there was silence. Then she answered dully, "All right, Patty." That was all. At a quarter past seven I knew she was already in bed.

"Bye, Mom."

As I opened the front door, I heard her call—as if she had been asleep and suddenly wakened—

"Wait a moment!" I was surprised to see her rushing downstairs in her flannel bathrobe. She came over to me and squeezed me in her arms.

"Good-by, Patty. Take good care of yourself."

"Sure, Mom," I answered, expecting something more. But she released me, turned, and hurried back upstairs. I didn't want to be late, and I hastened out, into the frosty night.

The Simpsons' house was warm and noisy. The five children ranged in age from ten to two years. They were a handful, clamoring for attention before I'd even removed my coat and snow-covered boots.

"Wait a moment, kids! Give Patty a chance to get in the door," Mrs. Simpson chuckled, rescuing me. Shortly, she and Mr. Simpson left.

At 9:30, when the two oldest were finally in bed, I had a moment to myself. Glancing out at our house, I thought about Mother. *Strange,* I mused, *she never made such a big deal about my going out before. Maybe she's getting better. I hope she'll stop crying so much.*

The Simpsons came home after midnight. Mr. Simpson watched from the porch as I left.

Once inside our house, I realized how hungry I was, and went into the kitchen to get something to eat. As I poured a glass of milk, something struck me as odd. There was an unusual humming noise. I stood very still and listened. It seemed to be coming from outside—something like an engine running. I opened the kitchen door and listened. Yes, it *was* a car engine. I looked down the driveway toward the garage. The doors were closed. I felt my throat tighten. Mother never closed them. I pulled on my coat and hurried down the driveway. I noticed smoke seeping out. My heart was racing as I pulled the heavy doors open. A cloud of smoke billowed around me, burning my eyes, choking me. It was Mother's car. The engine was running. I yanked open the door and found her slumped over the wheel.

"Mom! Come on! You have to get out!" I reached over her to the ignition key and turned off the engine. She didn't move. "Mom, wake up, it's me, Patty!" She stirred, groaning, as I dragged her from the car.

"Go 'way, leave me alone, . . ." she moaned.

"No, I won't" I pulled her roughly out of the garage and half carrying her limp body, got her into the house. By then I was coughing and crying.

She protested weakly. "Let me die. Please let me die." I propped her in a kitchen chair.

"Mom, I have to get the doctor," my voice was shaking.

"No," she said groggily. "Just get me some water. . . . I'll be all right . . . all right now."

I gave her a glass of water. Her hands were trembling, so I held it to her lips. She drank and coughed, and drank some more, then put her head down on the table. Long moments passed when I wondered if she was unconscious.

Then she started to weep softly. I sat down, shaken and relieved. I knew she would be all right.

"Why did you do it, Mom? Why? It's wrong. A mortal sin." As soon as the words were out, I knew it was the wrong thing to say.

"What difference does it make? My life is over," she said flatly.

"But *I'm* here. What about me?" I protested.

"Yes, Patty, I know. I'm sorry. Really I'm sorry. Let me go to sleep now. I'm all right" And then, "Patty, please, forgive me. . . . " She was pleading like a child.

I was torn between pity and outrage.

I helped her up to her bed, though she really did seem strong enough. She had stopped crying. Evidently, she had not been in the garage very long. After I was sure she was settled, I turned to leave, then hesitated at the door.

"Mom, I want you to know I love you."

She didn't answer.

"I love you, Mom. Okay?"

She had already fallen into a deep sleep.

My mother had survived the attempt to end her life, but in a real sense I had lost my mother. She was no longer able to care for the two of us. So, at sixteen, I took over as her guardian and felt responsible for her welfare.

For the next three months I was afraid to leave her alone at night. I turned down calls to baby-sit, and tried to make her stay up with me past seven o'clock. I was determined to change things. I urged her to talk to me and listened stoically as she poured out her anguish. Her spirit was broken. She had barely enough strength to get through her teaching day.

"I don't want anyone to know what's happened,

Patty," she confided her eyes startled with fear. "What would people say if they knew?"

"No one's going to know, Mama," I assured her. "No one has to know. And he'll come back soon."

"No, he won't! He'll never come back." Her voice was hard, the lines around her mouth more drawn. "And I wouldn't take him back. Not after this!"

I was angry with her, but I kept my anger under control. I felt like screaming, shaking her, but I knew I had to be very careful. I waited anxiously for the day when my brother would come home.

In late spring Ed returned. I was relieved, for now I had someone to share the burden. Several things happened during that time.

Of immediate importance to me was that Ed took up the daily task of protecting Mother.

When summer came, I felt a little freer and began babysitting again. We took Mother to the movies and for long drives in the country on the weekends. She went along passively, barely conscious of our efforts.

I was also grateful that I had Ed to talk to, though I could not bring myself to mention the attempted suicide.

"I don't know what's going to happen when you leave in September," I told him. "She gets—really bad."

"Don't worry, Patty," he assured me. "She's over the worst of it. This summer's been good for her. She'll come through." I hoped he was right.

Inwardly, I recognized a serious change in myself.

Ed and I went to church together. I didn't want to go, but was afraid to tell him. Church had suddenly become meaningless ceremony for me. I hadn't prayed since I was a little girl. It had done no good then, and seemed of no use now. There was no one listening.

In my innermost heart I doubted that God existed. And if He did exist, what did He have to do with me, or I with him? My father had been right, after all. Religion was an empty ritual for self-satisfied people. But I kept my thoughts to myself, because they frightened me with their empty, hopeless sound.

In September, Ed went back to the university and I began my last year in high school. My classmates were caught up in an aura of expectant excitement that I couldn't share. I wasn't hoping for a letter of acceptance from a college, nor was there a job waiting for me. I knew I would have to work, but I wasn't prepared for anything. My future faced a blank wall.

In gym class that fall I met Marge and we became fast friends. She was a tall, lanky, energetic girl with bright blue eyes and a sparkling wit—an irrepressible optimist. A family friend was an executive in a large New York corporation, and he promised Marge a job after graduation.

"There's a lot to do in the city, Patty. Why don't you get a job with me, and we'll do lots of things together. Shows. Museums. We'll have a ball."

I was enormously cheered by Marge's encouragement. For a moment I thought that maybe my future wasn't so empty. I began to dream about exciting times in New York City. Maybe there would be parties to go to, people to meet. Maybe there was something for me out there. Maybe an exciting, romantic, *someone*, too.

That fall was not without its shocks, however.

I came home from school one late November day and discovered my father's car in the driveway. It had been almost a year since he left. For a moment I was afraid to go into the house. Then I hoped he had come back, to work things out. Mother's wasn't home, so at least there wouldn't be a battle going on. I went in and found Daddy downstairs in the darkroom, packing his equipment into cartons.

"Hello, Patty. I came to get my things." There were deep lines around his mouth I had never seen before, a worn look. "How are you getting along?"

"I'm okay, Daddy. Are you going to be here? I mean, stay here for awhile?"

"No, I'm moving to Chicago. I've got a job offer that looks pretty good. Why don't you help me take some of these boxes to my car. . . ."

We worked silently together, loading up the trunk and the back seat. Soon the car was filled with his clothes, his camera equipment. Last, I carried out his fishing gear. We stood in the living room for a moment. My heart pounded.

"We didn't get to go fishing, did we?" I managed, awkwardly. I wanted to make him stay, make him see that I needed him.

"No," he answered, "I guess not." He put on his coat.

Gently, he put his hands on my head for a moment. "I want to get going. Before your mother sees me. I don't want any more scenes."

"Daddy—I'm graduating this year. Do you—could you—" I couldn't get the words out.

"I don't know where I'll be by then. But I'll keep in touch. As soon as this job works out, I'll send you some money. That's a promise. I've got to go now. Take care of yourself." He kissed my forehead quickly. And then he was gone.

I watched him get in the car—just as I had watched so anxiously as a little girl for him to come home. He drove away. He wasn't coming back.

But still I clung to a thread of stubborn hope, and

each day I came home from school and looked in the mailbox. He had said he would keep in touch, and maybe he would. Weeks went by, and there was no letter. Then one day a large envelope arrived for my mother. The return address showed the name of a law firm in Reno, Nevada. I put it on the coffee table and went up to my room to wait for her to come home. I was frightened. Something terrible was going to happen when she opened that envelope.

I lay down and drifted into a restless sleep. "Oh, no, no. O God, he can't do this!"

My mother's piercing cry woke me suddenly. I heard her sharp heels rushing down the upstairs hall to my room. The door flew open, and she ran in, her eyes glittering with rage. She threw a wad of typewritten pages on my bed and glared down at me.

"Do you see this? Do you see what your father's done? He's suing me for divorce! He wants to divorce me!" Her face flushed bright red as she paced fitfully across the room. "Well, he's not going to get away with it! I won't let him do this to me!" She hurled the words at me. "You'll see, he won't get away with this!"

I didn't know what to say to her. Her fury stunned me. "What can you do, Mom?" I asked timidly.

"Fight him, that's what I can do!" she shouted. She laughed, an ugly ragged sound. "We'll get a lawyer and we'll fight him!"

She sat down on the bed and grabbed my hand. "Don't worry, Patty," she said. "We'll stop him. We'll fight him all the way." She sprang to her feet. "I'm going to call a lawyer, right now." Her eyes narrowed, and her voice had a hard edge to it. "I'm going to make him regret the day he dared to humiliate me!"

She rushed out of the room and down the stairs to the living room. I got up and closed my door to muffle the shrill sound of her agitated voice. She was on the telephone. "Yes, I want to see him tomorrow! . . . I want an appointment tomorrow afternoon. . . . Yes, I'll be there at four o'clock."

We'll fight him, she had said. *Fight him,* I wondered. *Fight him for what? He's gone, and he's never coming back,* I thought, *and I don't want to fight. I just want to get away from here and never come back. Fight your own war, Mom,* I thought, as I lay down wearily. I'm not going to join your army. I wished that Ed were home. Maybe he'd know what to do.

I continued to draw on Marge's enthusiasm, as dry roots suck up even a breath of moisture. It was so good to have a real friend, too, one who didn't pry, even though I knew she could sense there was something wrong.

She could make the gloomiest day into an outrageous joke. We went to the movies, read the same books, went ice skating and spent long afternoons imagining how we could decorate our apartment.

It was Marge's confidence that I drew on, and her encouragement that was to alter my life. That spring, she coaxed me into trying out for a part in the school play. I was stunned when I was given a part. I was to play a brash, comical teenager whose impudent comebacks punctuated every scene. As we rehearsed, I discovered a strange freedom in taking on another identity, saying things I wouldn't dare to speak in real life. I felt charged with drive and sudden ambition that I didn't fully understand. Rehearsal became the central focus of each day.

On opening night, the crowd thundered its approval and we received five curtain calls. I bowed in the spotlights as the applause washed over us. I wanted it to go on. I felt almost dizzy with a heady excitement. For the first time, I was drunk with a sense of glory—importance.

I never imagined, as a high school starlet, that this craving would one day control me, like an insatiable thirst.

Three weeks after graduation, Mother and I were on a train, heading west for Reno, where Father hoped he would be able to get quick divorce. Mother's conversation with the other passengers was animated.

Sullenly, I turned away. Incredibly, she was enjoying herself, and silently I hated her. I had tried so hard to love her, to rouse her from apathy. I had failed. Only the prospect of battling my father in the courtroom seemed to revitalize her. I felt like a piece of luggage.

Mother's lawyer, an imposing, white-haired man, drove us to the courthouse the morning of the proceedings. We followed him into the judge's chamber, a dim, high-ceilinged room with empty straight-backed chairs waiting around a long dark table. The lawyer turned to me. "Patty, your mother and I are going into the courtroom now. You wait here until it's time for you to give your testimony." He smiled reassuringly. "It won't be long."

I sat alone in the room. The air smelled of stale cigars. From floor to ceiling, rows of leatherbound volumes guarded the walls in monotonous order. I stared at the inscriptions, but couldn't read them. They all looked the same, like faded headstones in forgotten cemeteries. Somewhere in the room a clock ticked.

The door opened, and a uniformed man led me

into the courtroom and told me to sit in the witness stand. He put a Bible in front of me and I swore to tell the truth. *How strange,* I thought, *to make a vow on a book I've never read.* I looked out over the rows of empty seats. Mother was at a table to the right with her lawyer. And there, on the left, was my father. I looked away quickly, but I could feel his eyes on me.

The questioning began. Is your mother considerate of you? Does she take care of you? Did she ever mistreat you? Spend money recklessly? Use foul language in your house? Alienate your father's family? Did she tear your father down in front of you? Did she get drunk? The questions went on, the answers required no thought. I was hardly conscious of my words. I responded in a steady monotone. I felt nothing but my father's gaze, like a weight on me.

At last it was over, and I was led back to the judge's chamber.

Leaning against the window frame, I felt my hands shaking. His gaze stayed with me, the memory of his tight-lined mouth.

Outside, the Nevada sky was a dazzling blue, so intense it hurt to look at it. Far off in the distance the pale jagged profile of mountain ranges stretched along the horizon. I wondered if I could find green forests there, rivers running into waterfalls that poured through valleys no human eyes had ever seen, primeval ground no foot had ever touched.

Mother burst into the room exultantly, with a torrent of words. "We won, Patty, we won! Patty, you did so well. It was because of you that we did it." She ran toward me with her arms spread out. I turned away from her. A floodgate broke inside of me.

"Oh, Patty, don't cry. It's all right now, honey. We won, dear, we won!"

I pressed my face against the window, and the mountains blurred.

What had we won? I felt only guilt, a suffocating sense of loss, and the desire to escape to a clean, untouched place where I could be someone else, anyone else, but me.

Chapter Four

The summer after the trip to Nevada, I was able to bury my unhappiness in the busy activity of my office job in New York. Marge and I worked in the same building, and commuted to work every day. We still hoped someday to be able to get an apartment in New York together, and she listened eagerly as I shared my dreams of traveling to faraway places. We loved the excitement of making new friends, and often had parties of our own at 309 Warwick Avenue on Saturday nights.

But perhaps the most satisfying times were those spent with a young man I had met through friends. Ray was a college student, and our casual times together during his school breaks had grown in frequency.

One night in August, Marge and I were hosting yet another Saturday night party. Before our friends arrived I made a last-minute inspection of the house. I had worked hard on it, hoping by its physical changes to chase away the specters of past memories.

As I walked through the downstairs I couldn't help thinking how wonderful it all looked. Night after night I had commuted home from work, and pulled on my paint-stained work clothes. I had stripped away the dingy wallpaper, and painted every inch of the eight rooms in a new harmony of color. Then I had the sofa and chairs reupholstered in warm golds and greens. Everything looked new and splendid. *Somehow,* I said to myself as I surveyed my creation, *this old house is going to live—we'll bury the dead.*

The party was spectacular. People poured in—few faces, familiar faces—laughter mingled with music, and liquor flowed into iced tumblers.

How I loved it all, the faces, sounds and colors, the triumph in my heart. I had *arrived.* I was somebody. All of those people filled the house because I drew them there.

Most important, Ray was there. I casually bumped into him and was at once swept into the comforting circle of his arms. It was like magic, and I was the sorceress who held the charms. And now Ray held me.

But always the morning came, when the house was still as death. My head ached on the pillow and a bitter nausea burned in my throat. I dragged myself downstairs to plow through the clutter of soiled glasses, littered plates, and empty cans. I cleared away the evening's rubble, trying to put things in order before Mother and Ed came downstairs.

Then I stretched out on the sofa to rest my aching head. I lay there staring at the silver loving cup on the mantle over the fireplace. Father had won it in a skeet-shooting contest. I wondered why he had left it behind. The room had lost its warming glow and my mind was swimming.

Somehow I was moving backward in time, half hung-over, half mesmerized with broken images. . . .

. . . dark water was pushing against me. I was tired and couldn't fight it . . . the water was cold, and the shoreline lost in darkness . . . I had to fight, had to keep swimming . . . my lungs were bursting . . . I wanted to cry out . . . there was no release from the current that swept me . . . Where are you? . . . Where are you? . . .

I was conscious of the room again, and shuddering with cold. My eyes were fixed on the loving cup. I got up, walked over to the fireplace, and took it down. Opening the hall closet, I thrust it into a box of old clothing. Then I went to the medicine cabinet and took two aspirin.

Later that day, Mother asked me, "Where's your father's silver cup, Patty? Don't tell me it got damaged last night?"

"No," I answered offhandedly. "I decided it doesn't go with the room. I have something better in mind."

The next day I bought a cut-crystal bowl. I placed it ceremoniously on the mantle, hoping it would exorcise any lingering, ghostlike memories. *You can't come back,* I mused silently. *You don't belong here anymore.*

The hangover passed, of course. I eagerly looked forward to a party the very next weekend, an "artsy" event in Greenwich Village. Marge and her boyfriend were going. I found myself increasingly preoccupied in my daydreaming moments with my frequent escort—Ray.

Ray was short, slender, with light wavy hair and an engaging smile that crinkled the corners of his gentle blue eyes. He was easy to talk to, easy to dance with, and that weekend, we left the party in Greenwich Village to huddle over hot coffee in a nearby diner.

He drove me home that night, and the next day

called to ask if he could see me again. I agreed, surprised to have captured his attention. Even more I was pleased that he made no demands and listened to everything I had to say. For me it was a warm and easy relationship.

Only occasionally did I catch a glimpse of a *different* Ray. At odd moments, he seemed uncomfortable, intense. Nothing I could put my finger on. I brushed it aside because I liked—even needed—the *other* Ray, the one who was so comfortable to be with. And besides, we were "just good friends." I had so many plans I needed to be free, to take a long trip with the money I had saved, to enjoy life.

For six months we saw each other whenever he returned from school. I swept him into the round of weekend parties and prowls through the New York night spots. He fit in easily, but I sensed something in him that held back. In some ways he seemed more settled than I, and I thought that perhaps the parties bored him a little.

But I wanted to move with the crowd, taste the excitement, feel the pulse of the music in every moment. There was never enough excitement for me, and I wanted it all.

On a quiet afternoon the following summer, Ray and I went for a drive in the country. We found a peaceful park overlooking the Hudson River. I knew I could no longer evade the questions I had seen in Ray's eyes. On a shaded bench, we sat down and Ray turned to me

"Patty, I want you to marry me. You know I love you and I want to spend my life with you."

I tried to stop him. "Ray, I can't make a decision life that just now. I can't. . . ."

"I know. I can wait. You can have all the time you need. I know you don't feel the way I do, but that's all right. Just give me a chance to show you what we can have together. I know we can have a good life."

"Ray, I can't settle down. There's so much to see in this world. I want to travel. Do things."

"There's nothing we can't do together, Patty. But I'm not going to pressure you. Just tell me you'll think about it seriously. I love you, Patty."

He looked so vulnerable, so sweet and helpless that my heart ached. I wished I could say, I love you, too. But I couldn't. He reached for my hand and I pulled away. I couldn't face him. My feelings were so mixed up. When I was with him I felt a hurt and fear and loss that came from some innermost recesses. He was good, so comforting, so real. What was wrong with me? Why couldn't I love him?

"I want to go home," I blurted. I couldn't stop the tears, and I was frightened. I didn't want to lose control in front of him.

"Patty, I'm sorry," he said gently. I could see that my reaction confused him. "What did I do? Don't cry."

He tried to put his arms around me, but I pulled away.

I laughed suddenly, a forced laughter. "I'll tell you what. Let's *go* somewhere, let's *do* something! Let's go to that place we passed down the road and have a drink. It's a beautiful day and we're supposed to have fun. Okay?

I could see that my swinging moods had totally confused him now. He took out his handkerchief and dried my tears.

"Sure." He looked at me intently. "I never want to hurt you, Patty. You mean everything to me."

"Fine. Let's go." I pressed my advantage. "I'm ready for a good time!"

We stopped at a road house for dinner. I ordered

one drink, then another. Slowly the evening blurred into dancing and laughter. But Ray's intent look haunted me.

In the morning I couldn't remember very much. My head ached fiercely and my mouth was parched. Wistfully, I wondered if I had had a good time. Surely. Didn't I always have a wonderful time?

Perhaps it was the pressure I felt in Ray's presence—or maybe just my ever-restless spirit. That March, I made my dream of traveling a reality. For four months I toured Europe, beginning with a leisurely cruise across the Atlantic. I climbed London Tower, strolled the Champs Elysée and the Bridge of Sighs, cheered matadors in Spain, swam in the Mediterranean and crossed the Alps.

The fantastic escape was over too soon it seemed. Before I knew it, I was back in America on a late June morning. Ed drove me home from the docks. All I could say to him was, "It's too soon to be over."

At home Mother threw her arms around me and hugged me close.

"Let me look at you, Patty," she said, cupping my face in her hands. "Yes, you're the same. None the worse for travel."

But something had changed, I thought, later that night as I lay in bed listening to the familiar night sounds. *I've changed. I can do what I want, go where I want. From now on I'm going to have excitement all the time. I'm going to do everything I want to do, see all the places. . . . And sleep overtook me.*

For the next year, I forced myself into the old routine: commuting to work, dating on the weekends, going to ballgames with Ed and Mother. But life had changed for me: The fear of commitment had finally caused me to break up with Ray, and Marge was married. A whirlwind courtship had resulted from one of our jaunts to a Dixieland jazz club in the city. She had met a young musician from California and within a few months was married and living in Manhattan. I stopped by for dinner occasionally, but it wasn't the same anymore. Others in our crowd were getting married and moving on. I would have felt abandoned, except for letters now coming from Europe.

During my travels in Germany, I had met an American soldier who was stationed in Frankfort. We were introduced through a friend who thought a stateside visitor might cheer up a draftee homesick for New York. I had liked Bert immediately. He was quick witted, darkly handsome, and lots of fun. He showed me the sights, cracked outrageous jokes about army life, had a wild imagination and an offbeat, hard-eyed view of the world that intrigued me. Underneath the wisecracks and seeming indifference, there was a quiet gentleness that I admired. His coolness toward his family's Jewish faith suited my indifference to religion. I could relax and be myself with him.

I looked forward to his letters, and answered them as soon as they arrived.

That correspondence was one of the few bright spots. Mostly I was lonely and bored. The working world was bleak and I longed to escape. I still went to parties, but somehow they had lost their glamor. I dreamed of travel, and began to save for the next great excursion. I determined I'd break free from the things that seemed to bind my spirit. I wouldn't live a caged existence.

By the following June, I was living in New York City in my own apartment. Tired of the commuting hours and feeling shut off from the center of life, I decided to rent the tiny apartment in Chelsea that Marge and her husband were vacating for larger quarters. It was furnished, inexpensive, and fulfilled my drive to be out on my own again.

But the new life was a lot different than I had thought it would be. The loneliness was more than I had bargained for. I was desperate for friends. The evening hours in the small room and a half filled me with a rising panic. I searched for ways to get out. I joined a swim club, went to poetry readings, had dinner with girls from the office and endured empty chatter. It seemed that something was waiting for me in the silence—and solitude became a terror.

And then one Friday evening in late summer the phone rang.

"Hi, there. What's a nice country girl like you doing in the big city?"

I couldn't believe it. I laughed in sheer delight. "Bert! It's you! Are you back? Are you really in New York?"

"Sure am. Home in the Bronx, to wander no more. May I turn into a spineless worm if I move ten paces from the Grand Concourse as long as I live. And how are you doing?"

"I'm fine. Will I see you soon?" I suddenly wanted to see him more than I'd ever wanted to see anyone in my life.

Evidently, he was just as eager to see me. After some light banter, he announced that he'd be on my doorstep in one hour.

I was filled with happy relief. With Bert's arrival, the crushing fear lifted. I wasn't alone. Everything would be fine.

Through the fall and winter, Bert and I saw each other constantly. We went to the movies, to the beach, walked through the park. I fixed dinners for him and enjoyed the new adventure of cooking for someone. I was happy with my life. Bert was planning to go back to college soon to complete his degree. I was planning another trip to Europe. He couldn't understand my enthusiasm.

"I don't want to go anywhere outside of the U.S.A.," he declared. "I'm so glad to be here, in crummy old New York, I could kiss the pavement."

I could not tell him, but the very thought of such a rooted existence terrified me. Though I was pleased when Mother and Ed met and liked Bert when he came home with me that Christmas, I was determined to keep him at arm's length. I was still racing inside, as if I were in a competition. I felt that I was chasing after an unknown *something* —or being chased.

In any case, my bank account was growing, and soon I'd be traveling again. Bert lightheartedly tolerated my obsession, and never tried to get threateningly close. Everything was splendid. Until Ed called me at the office one winter afternoon.

I hadn't been home for three weekends, and Ed said he wanted to talk to me. He sounded concerned.

The next Saturday, after dinner, Ed and I sat down in the living room to talk. Mother had gone to bed early. Ed was very serious and deliberate.

"A few weeks ago," he began, "Mother ran into an old friend. He'd seen Daddy recently at a photography show in New York. Seems he's living with Clara just outside of the city."

Ed paused a moment and gathered his thoughts. "Mom's been talking about him ever since then. She's full of remorse and she keeps rehashing the past. I'm worried about her, Patty."

"What can I do?" I was at a loss. I didn't want to think about the past either—about my father, or my mother's broken life. I didn't have any solutions for her and I couldn't tell Ed the truth—that I didn't want anything to do with it.

He got up and paced slowly across the room. "I was thinking, maybe—" He stopped and looked at me steadily. "I think you should get in touch with him."

"Me!" I shouted. "Why me? For that matter, why should any of us get in touch with him?"

"Mom needs something, Patty. Some hope. She can't keep going this way. She's so unhappy."

"And you think my getting in touch with him will give her hope? How? What can I do? Ask him to come back to her?" I laughed sharply.

Ed sat down next to me on the sofa, pleading. "How can we know if we don't try? Patty, I can't stay here forever. I can't be her guardian for the rest of my life."

So that's it, I thought angrily. *He wants out, so I have to pave the way.* In the next moment a surge of guilt went through me. He was right. I was free, after all, and he was trapped. It wasn't fair, and I knew it.

"Ed, why can't you see him?"

Ed looked away, his jaw set in a hard line. "It wouldn't do any good. We never got along. He never thought much of me."

And what does he think of me? I wondered, remembering my father's eyes in that Nevada courtroom three years before.

"He'll talk to you, Patty. I know he will. Maybe nothing will come of it, but isn't it worth a try? For Mother? For me? Patty, please!"

We talked for a long time, debating back and

forth. At last I agreed. I couldn't do anything else. Ed was asking for his freedom, and I had to try to help him. It seemed futile, but I agreed to a meeting with Father.

As I returned to the quiet of my apartment that night, I nearly panicked again. For a moment, I thought I glimpsed the ghost I had been trying to exorcise so long.

Chapter Five

Two weeks after my talk with Ed, a chilling winter rain poured down as I jostled my way through the rush-hour crowds on West 40th Street. Daddy had suggested we meet at the Hofbrau for supper. Entering, I looked around at the carved wooden booths with their red-checkered tablecloths. The place was old-fashioned, smelling of sauerbraten and beer. The thumping beat of a polka belted out from the jukebox.

I picked a booth near the door and sat down to wait for him. I felt tense, remembering our phone conversation. I had reached him at a photo processing lab in Queens, and when he answered I could hardly speak. Our words came out strained. After a long silence, he agreed to see me, and I hung up with an anxious foreboding. Every day since, I had wanted to call him back and cancel the appointment. But I wouldn't have been able to face Ed if I backed out. There was nothing to do but go through with it.

I glanced disinterestedly at the menu. Nothing appealed to me. I wasn't hungry. I was about to order a drink to calm my nerves, when I saw the waitress directing him to my table.

He tossed his raincoat on the empty seat and sat down across from me with a heavy slump.

"Hello, Patty. How long have you been waiting?"

My face felt flushed and my hands were shaking. I hoped he wouldn't notice.

"Just a few minutes, Daddy." I put the menu down nervously. "How are you?" I asked.

"Oh, not too bad." He called the waitress over and ordered drinks for both of us. His face looked bloated and sallow. His hair had thinned and there was a grim weariness in his movements. His dark gray suit showed wear and hung slack, unpressed.

Politely, he asked about me, making an effort to be affable. I knew he must be feeling as strained as I.

I told him about my apartment in Chelsea, my job, and the daily routines that filled up my life. Eventually, I launched into an enthusiastic description of my trip to Europe. The drinks arrived and I paused, sipping the beer to wash out the cotton that clung in my throat.

I fumbled in my purse for the collection of photographs I had taken with the camera I had bought in Germany, anxious to hear his appraisal. He went through them quickly, making comments about angles and light and composition, suggesting ways to crop and print that would improve the images. I waited eagerly for some words of encouragement. There were none.

"I really enjoy taking pictures, Daddy," I pursued hopefully. "Now I know why you find it so fascinating."

His mouth tightened into a hard line and he looked away from me. "It's a pretty dull racket. Doesn't pay worth a damn. I'm into the processing end of it, and believe me, there's nothing fascinating about it."

He ordered two more drinks, and launched into a dispirited monologue about his unsatisfying job, his difficult boss, the lack of opportunity. I slowly downed my second round, feeling lightheaded, but a lot more relaxed.

Through dinner, I chattered on superficially about restaurants in different countries, what the weather was like in England, the friendliness of the Italians, the cleanliness of the Swiss, anything to keep the conversation moving. He didn't seem to be listening. His eyes had a vacant look, as if he was having a hard time understanding what I was saying.

At last, when another round of drinks arrived, I began to talk about Ed and Mother.

"Mom's been talking about you a lot lately," I ventured. "She's been wondering how you're doing."

His eyes focused. "She needn't bother," he said coldly. "I'm doing fine without her."

Hastily, I tried to right things, though I couldn't imagine what I'd said that was wrong. "She's just interested, I guess, . . . " I offered lamely. A panic was cutting through my lightheadedness.

"There's nothing for her to be interested in," he said sharply. "I don't have any money, if that's what she's after. I'm broke, Patty. Do you hear me? Flat broke! That farce of a divorce trial in Reno took my last dime." He swallowed his beer quickly and slammed the glass down on the table. "So she may as well forget it. I have nothing more to give her."

"Oh, please, I didn't mean that. She isn't after money. . . . You don't understand," I stammered. How had I bungled such a simple mission as talking to my own father?

"I don't understand," he laughed harshly. "Oh

yes I do. I've had twenty years of your mother's spite! That's as much as I can take!"

He stood abruptly and reached for his raincoat. "I've got to get going. Do you take the subway?" It was obvious I was being dismissed, as if I were still a little girl.

Father paid the check and we walked outside into the cold air. He paused and looked away awkwardly down the busy street. Then he turned to me briefly. "Well, take care of yourself, Patty. I'm going to be traveling on business for the next few weeks. But I'll give you a call when I get back."

He kissed my cheek quickly and then vanished around the corner.

The chilling rain soaked through my damp coat and seemed to penetrate the center of my being. My head ached miserably. Shivering, I raced to the subway, wondering if I'd ever feel warm again.

When I went to Mother's house the following Sunday, Ed cornered me alone in the kitchen. "Well, what did he say, Patty? How did it go?"

I had dreaded this all week. Since the evening with Dad, I had felt drained and my body ached. I'd begun coughing, until my chest hurt.

I was irritated with Ed's demanding questions. "He didn't want to talk about Mom at all. He got very angry when I mentioned her and then he left. It's no use, Ed. I can't do anything about it."

"When will you see him again?"

"See him? I don't know. He said he'd call me in a few weeks. Please, let it alone." I knew I had failed. I didn't want to talk about it anymore. A weariness, a sickness was dragging at me."

"Excuse me," I said, brushing past him. "I have to lie down for a while. I don't feel very good."

I went upstairs and collapsed on a bed. Cold and

hot waves rushed over me alternately. I was exhausted.

At seven that evening Ed woke me. I tried to get up, but my legs were shaking. I fell back on the bed.

"Patty, what's wrong?" Ed asked with alarm. He sat down next to me and felt my head. "Good Lord, you're burning up. Just lie still."

He hurried out of the room, and returned with Mother. She put a thermometer in my mouth. The room was spinning and the cough racked my chest. Mother looked at the thermometer. "Oh, Patty, it's 103. I'm going to call the doctor."

I didn't care. I just drifted back into a fevered sleep.

And in that sleep my dark dream came to me again and again. Darkness and water. This dream was somehow coiled around me inside, holding me with a certain tenderness and terror, like a serpent. I could not escape its hold, its powerful, strangling hold.

At some indefinite time, I woke, slowly, drifting awake, like one rising up from deep waters.

I heard my mother's voice somewhere in the distance. "How is she doing? Is she any better?"

"Yes, she's past the crisis. Thank God for penicillin. Without it we might have lost her." I recognized our doctor's voice, warm and comforting. "Well now, I think she's awake."

"What time is it?" I croaked, looking about the room. I could not tell whether it was afternoon or morning. "Did I miss my bus?" I tried to get up, but I couldn't move. My arms would not support me.

"Lie still, Patty," Mother said gently. She put her hand on my forehead. "You've been very sick. But you'll be all right now. Won't she, doctor?"

"Yes, she will." He sat down next to my bed.

And now, something about the angle of light coming in the window told me it must be afternoon.

"Patty, you've got to recuperate now. Pneumonia takes a long time. Drugs get us past the crisis, but there's a lot of mending to do now. How's the chest feel?"

"It hurts. Every muscle feels sore. I'm so tired, I can't get up."

As the doctor packed his medical bag, he continued talking. I was astonished to learn that I'd been delirious with fever for six days. I had no memory of time passing; everything was a blur.

"Nearly a week?" I gasped, my head rolling back on the pillow. "I can't believe it."

"It's true and you're staying right where you are for several more weeks." The doctor paused at the door. "I've left a supply of medicine, and I'll check on you tomorrow."

He left the room with Mother. I looked around at the walls I had scraped and painted blue, the familiar white curtains I had made myself. The daylight was fading. I was grateful to be home, in my own bed.

Grateful that, for a time at least, I was free from the horrible struggle.

Winter slowly passed into spring and just as slowly I regained my strength. The days were leisurely, and I read a lot. More important, my sleep was untroubled. For once, I really felt cared for; someone's responsibility.

I had given up the apartment, and it would be many weeks before I could return to work again. It didn't worry me. It was too much effort to think about the future. Just to be able to breathe without racking pain was an enormous relief. From time to time, vague memories of my meeting with my father came into my mind, but I turned them away. I was too tired to think about him.

One day a letter came, forwarded from my Chelsea address. It was a brief note from my father. I read it privately.

It said, "I'm moving to Florida next week. Got a pretty good job offer in Fort Lauderdale. Take care of yourself. I'll write when I have an address. Love, Dad."

That was all. There was no return address.

I tore up the note. I didn't want Mother to see it. What did it matter now? He wasn't important, not anymore.

But somewhere inside a voice accused. It must have been my fault. Something I said wrong. I must have driven my father away.

Chapter Six

During my months of recuperation, Bert came to see me every weekend. He had started his classes and was doing well. A homey charm drew me to him, and when I was strong enough, Ed loaned us his car to drive around town on sunny afternoons. Occasionally, we took in a movie.

Gradually, I found that I cared deeply for Bert. I was grateful for his constant warmth, his easy good humor. Over those slow months I realized that he was important to me. His constant reassurance filled a part of me that suddenly longed for permanence. Even when I went back to work, back to my independent life, the feeling did not leave. We met almost daily for lunch. Before I fully knew what I was doing, we began to talk about marriage, tentatively at first, then with a growing awareness that we wanted to make a real commitment to each other. It all seemed to fall into place during one otherwise casual lunch conversation.

"With my G.I. Bill and your salary," Bert reasoned, we could just about get by. We could find an inexpensive place in the Bronx. I think we can make it."

I was amazed to hear myself say, "So do I, Bert. I really do."

And in that moment, I realized that my dreams of travel weren't important any longer. I wanted desperately to have someone to care about, someone to fill the empty places.

When we broke the news to Mother, she wasn't at all surprised. "Well, you'll have a bit of a struggle until Bert is through school," she said. "But you're young and you can do anything when you're young." Ed gave his approval and Bert's family reacted to our decision without protest, even though we both knew they would have preferred that he marry a Jewish girl. They made a determined effort, however, to welcome me and to respect Bert's choice.

We were married in City Hall a few months later. For eight weeks we lived in a tiny sublet apartment in the Village, and in the fall of 1954 we took a more spacious apartment in the Bronx. I made curtains, painted walls, and filled the windows with house plants. I was happy, confident that the future held the abundant life I longed for.

One evening, four months later, Ed called me. I hadn't talked with him in two weeks, I had been so busy with the apartment. "Hi, Ed. You've got to see what we've been doing with this place!" I beamed.

Anxiety riddled his voice. "Patty, I want you to come home this weekend."

"I am home, Ed," I laughed, trying to ease the tension. "*This* is my home now."

"You know what I mean," he said impatiently. "Mother's not well. Something's very wrong. She's having a problem with her legs. They're covered with a rash."

"That doesn't sound very serious," I responded.

He was getting angry. "She isn't herself! Patty, please come out tomorrow."

Bert and I had plans to go to a party on Saturday, our first evening out in weeks. We'd also had our first little lovers' spat, and needed the time together. I was annoyed, but I couldn't refuse. I told him we'd be out the next day, even though I was sure Mother was fine.

When we arrived the next day, however, I saw that she wasn't fine. She was lying on the sofa, her face a pale mask.

"Mom, has the doctor seen you?" I asked anxiously.

"I have an appointment this afternoon." she said. "I'm so tired all the time. And my legs hurt so terribly that I have to teach sitting down these days. I've never done that in my life."

"I'll get lunch, Mom. You just stay put." I went into the kitchen and started preparing sandwiches, glad to have something to do to ease my growing worry.

Ed was right on my heels. "I called the doctor. He sounded very concerned. He told me he wanted to see her today. So I'm taking her over to his office at two o'clock."

Ed and Bert and I all made the trip to the doctor's office along with Mother. After she'd been in the examining room for a full hour, the doctor came out alone and sat down. He spoke slowly, choosing his words carefully.

"I wish I could tell you what's wrong, but I can't. The symptoms can mean any number of things. The only thing I'm sure of is that she belongs in the hospital, and right away. I don't want to waste any more time."

His urgency frightened me. "Doctor, she's never sick. What could be wrong?"

"That's what I want to find out, Patty. I'm going to make arrangements to admit her today. She's frightened, so we'll have to reassure her that it's just a precaution." He got up and went back to his desk to call the hospital.

Within the hour Mother was checked into a hospital room. I sat by her bed and held her hand. Her eyes were wide with fear and my heart ached for her.

"Patty, what's wrong with me?" Her voice was a thin whisper.

"They're going to find out, Mom. That's why you're here," I said with feigned confidence. "You'll be home in no time."

I did not know when we left the hospital that evening that Mother would never go home again.

Three months later, as we sat with the doctor in his office, I could see the discouragement in his face. He had been battling a degenerative disease in her connective tissue.

"We've done all we can, and that has been very little, I'm afraid. The disease is wasting her away. She hasn't responded to the cortisone treatments and we have nothing else to offer. I'm so sorry."

"What will happen to her?" I asked, dreading the answer.

"I think it would be best to find a comfortable nursing home for her. Our only chance is a spontaneous remission. But I can't hold out much hope. Her condition has deteriorated so drastically."

"Where should we take her?" Ed asked.

"I'll see what I can arrange," he assured us. "For now, just keep praying for her."

Pray, I thought bitterly. I had given it up so many years before.

The doctor found a nursing home in the Bronx. And over the next year, I watched Mother descend slowly, torturously toward a miserable death. Her weight dropped to eighty-three pounds and her hair turned pure white. I sat by her bed for long hours and held her bony hand. She was barely conscious during the last months. I listened to her whimper and groan, and thought about my father, somewhere in Florida. I felt a cold rage. *He's probably fishing, having the time of his life.*

When Mother died in November, I was glad that her suffering was over. Watching her die had led me into a pit of depression so deep I couldn't find my way out.

Ed and I put the house on the market and he moved to the city. When the house was sold some months later, a hard resentment took hold of me and wouldn't let go. I wrestled with impossible questions about my mother: Why hadn't I been able to do more for her? Why should I feel guilty? Why had she died? So much was unresolved.

At the same time, things were beginning to sour in my marriage. My old restless spirit was back. I was terrifyingly bored. It was as if I had gotten on a train, only to find it was carrying me the wrong way. But it was too late to get off.

Bert studied constantly for his classes. "That's all I've got time for now," he would say, without even looking up from his books. He was annoyed with me, and I felt guilty because I'd begun to nag him. But I couldn't seem to stop myself.

I made a special shopping trip for his birthday that year and found several beautiful shirts for him. But when he opened them he looked displeased.

"What's wrong?" I asked. "Don't you like them?"

"I prefer to buy my own clothes," he said.

His reply tore me up inside. I wanted to scream, to shake him out of his growing indifference.

One night I walked to the closet and put on my coat. "I'm going to the store," I said abruptly to the form hunched over a stack of papers. "Be back in awhile."

I walked down to the corner delicatessen and bought a six-pack of beer.

I went back to the apartment, took a glass from the kitchen, closed myself in the bedroom. Pouring myself a drink, I thought, *This will help me relax.* I drained the glass, and in a few minutes the sharp edges inside me began to dissolve.

I stretched out on the bed to watch images flicker across the television screen. There was nothing but an old "grade B" movie. I didn't care. I was comfortable; the pain was eased. I poured another can of beer into my empty glass. *Never fear,* I chuckled, repeating a motto from bygone party days, *no booze shortage here!*

I never saw the end of the movie. I never did on those nights. When Bert came into the bedroom, the television was playing to a silent house. Hours before, I had slipped into dreamless oblivion.

The therapist's office on East 66th Street was tastefully furnished with large, comfortable wing chairs, Currier & Ives prints and a black leather sofa against one of the walls. Even though I had initiated the sessions, I did not know why.

"What do you expect from therapy?" the therapist asked quietly. He was a tall, lanky man in a tweed jacket. His hornrimmed glasses gave him the look of a college professor. I squirmed in the wing-back chair.

"I don't know what to expect. I'm just unhappy. Unhappy with the way my marriage is going. With everything, I guess."

"From what you've told me," he pursued, "there seems to be a connection between your mother's death last year and this depression."

"Yes, I suppose so."

"We'll have to explore, of course. It takes time to get to the root of these things. Have you been taking any medication?"

"Oh, no, nothing." The thought of taking drugs frightened me.

"We'll, I don't think it's necessary. This is probably related to the grief process." He opened his appointment book. "I can see you on Tuesdays and Thursdays at five thirty. Will that be convenient?"

"Yes, I guess so," I said reluctantly. If only it *were* convenient. Neatly packaged. I felt like I was slowly coming unwrapped, and there was no way to stop it.

"Very good." He got up and ushered me to the door. "I'll see you next Tuesday, then, five thirty!"

On the subway going home, I fought back that old rising panic. And a hundred conflicting voices inside.

When the train pulled into my station I climbed wearily up the stairs to the street. Once on the sidewalk, the traffic and the crowds seemed to press in on me. And then there was our dull, routine little apartment—Bert and his blasted books. I wanted to escape. I clamped my lips tight to suppress a scream. . . .

Shaking, I hurried to the delicatessen on the corner. *I know what I need,* I said to myself. From the cooler, I picked out two six-packs.

That night, while John Wayne led the massive herd of cattle across a great river, I had already crossed into oblivion.

I saw my therapist twice a week for nine months—and I felt no better. In fact, many evenings I went out of his office more depressed than when I went in.

"It takes time, Pat," he reminded me, lighting his pipe. "I told you that when we started."

"I still feel awful most of the time. Maybe therapy isn't for me."

"What would you suggest?" he asked calmly.

He annoyed me. "How should I know?" I snapped. "You're the therapist!"

"And you're the patient."

"That's great. Really profound."

"You're very defensive, Pat," he observed coolly. "You use your anger to hide your feelings."

"Oh? And what feelings am I hiding?" I asked sarcastically.

"They're your feelings, Pat. You tell me."

"We're not getting anywhere," I exploded. "I feel like quitting this whole thing."

"How will that help?" he asked, puffing calmly on his pipe.

"It would save me a lot of money I'm wasting here!"

We wrangled on through the hour. Finally, I said, "Bert suggested that I take a class at the college."

"Do you want to do that?" Dr. Webster asked.

"Maybe I do. Maybe I could take a literature course. I might like that."

"That sounds like a good idea," he answered.

I was amazed. It was the first time in months he'd ever said anything decisive.

The next week I registered for a course in English literature. I dashed into the apartment that evening with an armload of books, excited and a little nervous. "Do you really think I can handle this?" I asked Bert.

"Yes. I told you I thought it was a great idea. Give you something to do. Better than hitting the booze every night."

Red lights went on. "I don't hit the booze every night!" I shot back. "It's only when I'm bored—and depressed."

He had opened a textbook and I'd lost him already. "I've got to cram for another two hours. Got a test tomorrow."

Yes, it will be better, I thought, making my way into the kitchen. *Maybe we won't have so many arguments.*

I took a can of beer out of the refrigerator and disappeared into the bedroom with a book. *I'll just have one drink,* I said to myself, *just to relax.*

I loved everything about going to school. I loved the reading, the exams, the papers, the vibrant discussions in class. When the term ended, my spirits sagged. But when my grade arrived, I was soaring. I'd gotten an A.

"Bert, I did it!" I exclaimed happily.

"You're into it now," he smiled. "Keep going."

He was completing his degree that month and would be doing graduate work in the evening. He had accepted a job teaching in a local high school starting in the fall. We would have more income. Everything was looking up. I no longer felt the need to visit the therapist. The evening my grades arrived, I poured myself a drink to celebrate my victory and salute good times to come.

I had been a matriculated night student for two years, welcoming the creative atmosphere of the college classroom. I even daydreamed about becoming a teacher, the one who stood before befuddled students and dispensed wisdom and knowledge.

One night as a Lit professor brought the class to a close, he stopped me as I was leaving the room.

"That last paper was excellent, Mrs. Zimmerman. Well-written and thought out. You have a keen mind for literature. Have you considered graduate work?"

"I've got three years of undergraduate work to finish first!"

"I hope you'll consider going to school full time," he said. "You really should. And I hope to see you back here next fall."

"Thank you," I smiled, glowing with praise.

I was floating on a cloud as I walked down the school corridor and out the door. I was eager to tell Bert what the professor had said to me.

As I waited for my train, dreaming about the bright future, I glanced across the station where a tall, heavyset man was standing reading a newspaper. He was wearing a rumpled raincoat. The dim light fell across his thinning grey hair. His face was barely visible, but something in the slope of this brow, the way he held his head made my heart catch in my throat. I stood, frozen to the spot. The train roared into the station as I cried out.

"Daddy!"

The subway doors slid open. He disappeared inside and the train rumbled away.

I was numb when I stumbled into the apartment.

"What's wrong?" Bert asked anxiously. "You look like you've seen a ghost."

"Maybe I did!" I sank into a chair. "I think I saw my father in the subway."

"But didn't he move to Florida?"

"That's the last I heard. He never wrote to me." The hurt in my voice betrayed the hard set of my jaw.

I got up and went into the kitchen. "Right now I need a drink." Bert came and stood in the doorway.

My hands were shaking as I filled the glass. "I

don't even know if it was my father. It just looked like him." I emptied the glass, and poured another. In my mind's eye I could see Mother, dying a painful death without the man she had continued to need so much.

"As far as I'm concerned," I said bitterly, "he's dead and buried. So it doesn't matter who it was in the subway tonight."

"Why don't you get some sleep?" Bert suggested. "You've had a rough day."

"I know. I'll come to bed in a few minutes. I want to relax for a bit." Bert opened his mouth to say something, then stopped. I'm sure he knew that if he mentioned my drinking we'd wind up in a fight. And we'd been fighting too much lately.

Suddenly all the excitement brought on by the professor's compliment was gone. Miserably, I poured another drink and sank into a chair. I found myself talking to the man I'd seen in the subway—whoever he was.

Guess what, Daddy, I'm going to college now. I'm going to be a teacher. Aren't you proud of me? I laughed out loud as I finished off the bottle.

That fall I did not go back to school.

Chapter Seven

One very important event occurred that cemented my decision to leave college. I got pregnant.

When I knew for sure, I threw myself into Bert's arms, more excited than I'd ever been in my life. "We're going to have a baby!"

He was as overwhelmed as I. "Did the doctor say when?"

"In May. I'm so happy! I hope it's a boy. But a girl is nice, too. Oh, what do you think, Bert?" I was a jumble of emotions.

"Either one will be just fine," he smiled, holding me. "It's going to be wonderful."

And it was wonderful. The nine months were a time for peace and joyful anticipation. I loved getting the baby's room ready, and buying maternity clothes. Hope and vitality burned within. I didn't need drinks to relax in the evening. I knew the baby would be perfect and beautiful.

Christopher was born in May, healthy and sound, everything I'd hoped he'd be. I was brimming with love for him and for Bert. My life was full.

I nursed the baby, bathed him, wheeled him in the carriage, and willingly let his small being take over my life.

But slowly, imperceptibly, the joy faded. It diminished somehow in the everyday routine.

One evening when Bert was teaching night school and Chris was sleeping peacefully in his crib, I found myself sitting at the kitchen table, pouring one drink after another—*just to relax,* I told myself. Somehow it was getting harder to kid myself, and I nearly forced myself to stop. I even put my hand on the bottle to push it away. And I thought, *Just one more. I won't let this happen again.*

But it did happen again. Again and again, beginning early in the evening, I longed for Chris's bedtime when I could sit down alone with a drink. I tried to keep it hidden, drinking only on the nights Bert was at school. I knew I wasn't fooling him. We just never talked about it.

Trying to jar myself out of this latest depression—and the drinking that was slowly overshadowing my life—I decided to go back to school. I needed the intellectual stimulation, I told Bert, and a goal to pursue. After all, I did want the degree, and I could manage two evenings of classes a week. And so I returned to school, back to writing papers, taking exams, and making plans. I loved meeting new students, exchanging ideas. And so what, I reasoned if I had a few drinks when I got home late from class. It was only because I was tired and wound up from the evening's exertion. It wasn't a problem, not really.

The months fled past me. Chris grew into a delightful toddler. I added more credits toward my degree. We moved to a larger apartment. I kept on drinking.

And then one night a phone call from Ed broke the mesmerizing sameness of my life. He was in the hospital for some tests.

"What kind of test?" Bert asked when he got home from school that night.

"He's had a heavy, persistent cough for the past two months." I realized that I hadn't seen Ed for two months. "I can't imagine what's wrong. He's never complained about not feeling good. He wants me to go down to the hospital tomorrow."

"Do you want me to go with you?" Bert asked.

"I think I'll go down in the afternoon. Maybe I can talk to his doctor."

"Don't worry. He's young and strong. Probably nothing serious."

Perhaps. But why could I not shake off the cold hand of a specter that seemed to grip me. That night, I drank even though Bert was home to watch me with his disapproving look.

Ed was sitting in a chair in his hospital room when I arrived the next afternoon. He was wearing a bathrobe and nervously smoking a cigarette. I tried to hide the shock I felt when I looked at his drawn face and glassy eyes. I could see how frightened he was, and I didn't want him to know that I recognized his fear.

Kissing him quickly, I sat down. "How are you doing?" I said, determined to be cheerful.

"I don't know how I'm doing. The doctor isn't saying very much. I want to get out of here. We're going away over the Fourth of July and that's next week.

"I'm sure you'll be out in a few days," I assured him.

"It's this constant cough and the chest pains, Patty." He put out his cigarette. "I couldn't sleep and I lost my appetite." His robe slid open a little and I noticed how thin his chest looked, his ribs protruding.

"Has the doctor done tests yet?"

"Tomorrow," he answered, glancing nervously from the bed to the window.

We chatted a little more, about nothing. Chatted just so our voices would fill the void fear had opened, and to fill a little time until, relentless, "tomorrow" would come with its verdict.

Leaving the hospital, I resolved to call Ed's doctor in the morning. I was worried. I'd never seen Ed so upset. He was usually in such control of his emotions.

In the morning, my phone conversation was brief. There was nothing to learn until the tests were complete, and all the results confirmed. When Bert and I visited the hospital again, Ed seemed less agitated.

"I'll only be here until Thursday. And the doctor says I'll be able to go away next weekend. I can't wait to get out of this place."

"How does your chest feel?" I asked.

"Better," he declared. "This was unnecessary, really. I should never have let the doctor talk me into it."

Later, at home, I sat quietly in the living room, lost in thought. Bert noticed, and asked me, "What is it, Patty? You look worried."

"It's nothing, I was just remembering mom, how sick she was. How frightened."

He put his arms around me. "Come on, let's get some sleep. I'm sure Ed's going to get a clean bill of health."

The following Tuesday, Ed's doctor called me. "Would you come down to my office, Mrs. Zimmerman? I'd like to talk to you about your brother." Hastily we set an appointment.

The next day I sat in his office, listening to the

quiet hum of the air conditioner, listening to the pounding of my own heart, because I couldn't grasp the meaning of what he was telling me.

"The cancer is beyond surgery. His lungs are past repair and I'm afraid it's gone through his entire system."

"It can't be. It can't be. He's only thirty-five. He wasn't even sick."

"I know, Mrs. Zimmerman. It runs wild in young people, and once it gets started, it just doesn't stop."

"How long does he have? How many months?"

He looked crestfallen. "Not months, Mrs. Zimmerman. Weeks. Maybe four to eight at best. I haven't told him. I think it would be unwise," he added softly. "I don't think it would help him to know."

"What will you tell him?" I asked, my eyes stinging with tears.

"We're telling him it's an 'unidentified virus that's difficult to treat.'" His eyes held a deep sadness. "I don't want to take away his hope. It's all he has now."

The next weeks were a waking nightmare. I went to see Ed in the hospital and kept up a cheerful front. I put off his probing questions, talked about the day he'd be out of the hospital. He failed rapidly. Each day it was more difficult for him to breathe. Soon, he stopped asking questions. When he stopped asking, I knew he knew the answer.

A few weeks before he died, Ed looked at me with imploring eyes. In a hoarse trembling whisper, he said, "The nurse here tells me to pray. Do you think it's all right? I don't go to church anymore. . . ."

"Of course it's all right. Yes, you should pray." I didn't believe what I was saying. For years I had not only avoided religion, but scorned it.

When the doctor told me the end was near I knew I would have to notify relatives, people I hadn't seen for years. That night I called my father's cousin Millie in Brooklyn. I had not seen her in a long time. She was grieved to hear the news and told me she would call other relatives. I didn't ask about my father and she didn't mention him. I was relieved. I didn't want to think about him. Certainly not then.

The next evening I was sitting in the hospital day room, taking a break from the long vigil at Ed's bedside. A voice startled me.

"Hello, Patty."

I looked up. There was my father standing next to my chair. I gasped audibly, because I could not believe my eyes. He sat down next to me.

"Millie called last night and told me about Ed. I came over, but I didn't go in to see him. I thought if he saw me, he'd know."

"He's not conscious, anyway," I replied sharply, "so it wouldn't matter now. He wouldn't know you were there."

He looked old and worn out. There was an aura of shabby defeat about his appearance.

"Are you living in New York?" I asked, a little more gently.

"I'm in Queens. I came back from Florida last year. Couldn't stand it there. I'm working where I was before. Same old job."

We sat in silence. Finally I said, "I'm sorry, Daddy, it's hard for me to talk right now." I turned away from him. I didn't want him there. I wanted him to leave. He seemed to read my thoughts.

"Well, I'll go along now. Here's my phone number. Give me a call and let me know how things are going."

"Yeah, sure. Thanks for coming."

He left the room. I wanted to rage after him. *Why show up now—like some sort of vulture, or death angel?*

I went home, hoping I could cry that night. The tears wouldn't come. I drank myself to sleep.

Ed died on Labor Day. My father came to the funeral. We talked stiffly for a few moments after the service. He said he would call me. I knew he wouldn't and I was glad to see him go. I didn't want to see him again.

In some ways, Ed's death swept my life clean. All of my childhood family was gone—since Father was like a cancer that I, at least with my conscious mind, cut out. Now I had only Bert to lean on.

And some new changes thrust me toward what I hoped was a new life, free from the past. With the money I received from Ed's life insurance, we were able to buy a small summer cottage on a lake in Connecticut. It hurt me that Ed was gone, but this cottage, in a way his final gift to us, offered beauty, serenity and the change I so craved. I became pregnant again, and a sweet baby girl, whom we named Jennifer, came into our lives.

Even as I pieced together a bright future, I could not see that I was like a cripple leaning on an unsteady crutch. And that crutch was about to break.

Chapter Eight

It was amazing how the momentum of routine, how the sheer force of days and years passing gave me the illusion that I was living. In the years after Ed's death, I surrounded myself with all the good things I thought I wanted from life.

One warm summer morning in 1969, I stood at the window of our newly built, waterfront home in Connecticut. Slowly our rocky financial situation had improved. And now, I was proud of our home with its tall stone fireplace, cathedral ceiling, and vaulted windows.

Drawing back the curtain, I looked out over the lawn, the flowering shrubs, toward the wide expanse of lapping waters. There, Chris and a friend were having a diving contest off the float. At age ten, Chris had grown into a sturdy, bright boy. And closer to me on the lawn, Jennifer was hard at work in her sandbox, putting all of her four-year-old inventiveness into a sand castle. They were beautiful children, and I felt a certain happiness that we had been able to give them such an idyllic childhood.

I let the curtain drop back. Yet, that was the problem. Everything was in place. From looking at the externals, I had a beautiful life. *Then why,* I thought, as I padded across the carpet toward the kitchen, *do I feel like I'm dying.*

I sat down at the kitchen table. This feeling crept up on me all too frequently, and I was becoming less and less able to deal with it. I felt dead in the midst of my own busy days.

Mentally, I reviewed my life. I was a good mother, gently urging Chris off to the bus, and then rushing Jennifer over to nursery school, which she seemed to enjoy. Then I took off my "mother badge" and became a student, diligently taking notes as I studied toward my degree—a goal I had decided to pursue once again. Why with so much seeming joy and purpose, did I feel it necessary to stop by the liquor store almost daily for my evening's supply? I did not dwell on that question very long. The problem *had* to be something else. Maybe Bert.

I got up and rummaged in the refrigerator. It was nearly noon, and I began to fix sandwiches for Chris and Jennifer. *Bert.* My thoughts were still rolling. *Why have we drifted apart?* I had hoped that the permanent move from the city to Connecticut would make a difference for us. It wasn't that we fought. We rarely talked to each other at all. Perhaps that was why he stayed in New York two nights a week, despite his reasoning that it cut down on the number of long commutes.

Maybe if he'd get a job in Connecticut, I thought, pouring glasses of milk. *Maybe if we could get some counseling.* This was a new game I was playing: Maybe if. I had to stop it. I opened the refrigerator to put the milk away. There was the ever-handy six pack. *Maybe if . . .* the inner voice began. I slammed the door shut.

I walked to the open window and called Chris

and Jennifer in for lunch. Dripping wet and sandy, they trooped inside as Chris's friend trotted home. I set their sandwiches and milk in front of them, and they hungrily devoured the food. I was pleased that they had healthy appetites, pleased that I was nourishing their young bodies.

Opening the refrigerator again, I pushed aside a few containers, looking for something that appealed to me for lunch. Lately, I had lost interest in food, even though I was so active. Just a bite here, or a hurried sandwich there. Instead, I reached for the six pack. It was summer, after all, and warm.

While my children rambled on about sandcastles and swimming lessons, I leaned against the sink smiling and nodding. I poured down another beer and felt like the dead among the living.

During that time, I even tried to stop drinking. For days and sometimes weeks, I would fight the craving to drift away in the soothing dimness of alcohol. I could hold out for a while, and then my resolve would break and I would rush for a drink.

Each morning, I looked at my face in the mirror as I brushed out my hair. I loathed what I saw. Not just the puffiness, but something visible to the eye. *When will this end?* I asked the frightened face that stared back at me. *Never,* came the reply.

The following spring I completed my degree. What should have been a time of fulfillment and joy was the beginning of the worst depression I had ever experienced. In desperation, I cried out for help the only way I knew how: I closed myself in my room to drink my way into oblivion.

How long did it go on? A few days, a week, I couldn't remember. I remembered screaming for help. I remembered Bert's taking me to the psychiatrist and I remembered pleading with him to put me in the hospital. For three days and nights I took the tranquilizers they gave me and lay on a bed in a small, bare room. On the third day, I walked out of the hospital. There was no help for me there. I asked Bert to take me home.

When I faced the psychiatrist again, he looked confused. "Why did you leave the hospital, Pat? You asked to be admitted," he reminded me.

"Yes, I know." I was so tired I could hardly speak. "I left because they can't help me. No one can help me. They don't know what's wrong with me."

"What is wrong, Pat?"

I took a deep breath. "I drink, doctor. A lot. That's what's wrong with me!"

He sat quietly. Then he said, "That's not surprising, Pat. These depressions are very acute, very dangerous." He leaned forward and smiled, reassuringly. "I'm sure, after we've gotten to the root of the problem, after you've ironed out these problems with your marriage, the drinking will stop. It's a symptom of the underlying disorders."

"*No,*" I shouted at him. "You've got it all wrong! If I can't stop drinking, nothing's going to change. And I can't stop!"

He continued to reassure me, with phrases that sounded like they were being read from a psychology textbook. I wasn't listening. After a while, he stopped talking.

"There's no hope," I said dully.

"We'll talk about this some more next time," he answered.

I left his office and hurried to my car. I needed a drink. I needed lots of drinks.

That fall I enrolled in graduate school. I didn't have any hope that going to school again would make a difference in my life. I didn't know what else to do. I dragged myself through the classes listlessly, wrote papers that didn't interest me and, after two semesters, I dropped out. I stopped seeing the psychiatrist, because our sessions were going nowhere.

In the spring, I embarked on a plan born of desperation. I decided to get a full-time job. I had not talked to Bert about my decision for one reason: I was planning to earn my own way, be independent, get out of the living death my marriage had become.

I found a job in a local corporation, researching and writing presentations for relocating executives and their families. I tried to plunge into the job with enthusiasm, determined to use this new ticket to freedom. My optimism was short lived. Within a month, I was drinking every night. I couldn't get through a day without alcohol. I kept on going to work, but I was utterly defeated. I was dying and I wanted to die.

I gave up the struggle.

I don't know why I went to the church service that particular Sunday. I awoke that morning with the usual pounding head and a sick feeling in the pit of my stomach. Bert had taken the children out for the day. I was alone.

I hated being alone, and wanted to get out of the house. No stores were open yet, and when I passed by the church, I decided to stop. Turning the car around, I pulled into the parking lot. Then made my way quietly inside the back door so no one would notice me. *This is as good a place as any to nurse a hangover,* I thought, as I slipped into a seat in the back of the room.

After a brief introduction, a large, smiling man in his forties took the podium.

"Good morning. I'm glad to be here. In fact, it's a

miracle every day of my life, that I can say 'good morning' to anyone." He looked out at his audience. "By rights, I shouldn't be here at all. In the natural course of events, I would have been dead long ago. You see, I'm an alcoholic and, ten years ago, there was nothing I wanted more than to die."

His words caught me by surprise, roused me from my stupor. I could not believe what I was hearing.

"I haven't had a drink in ten years. I've returned from a living death and I'm here to tell you how it happened."

He described his slow descent into uncontrolled drinking, his harrowing life in the service, the bizarre, violent episodes that riddled his career and his marriage. He recited a litany of catastrophes that bore no relation to my life. Yet, he was telling my story. The feeling of impending doom, the hopelessness and despair, the torment of alcoholic drinking that was consuming my life. I knew it all, I lived it every day.

"And then I found a fellowship of recovered alcoholics who had learned to stay sober, to live without a drink, one day at a time." His words reached out to me with flickering hope as he described his gradual ascent into the world of the living.

I listened, watching him closely as he invited questions from the audience. Hands were going up all over the room.

Responding to a young man who was sitting right in front of me, the speaker said there was an alcoholism council right there in town. "Once the alcoholic admits defeat, the doors of recovery can open wide," he said assuredly. "Help is there for the asking.

I didn't stop to speak to anyone when I left that morning. Thoughts were racing through my mind as I drove home. *Could it be possible,* I thought. That man was certainly real. I heard him, saw him in the flesh. He said he was an alcoholic and he recovered. Maybe I didn't have to die.

But as I walked into the empty house, a wave of despair broke over me. *I can't get through a day without a drink.* I went into the bedroom and sat down next to the telephone. How could I fight it? Could someone really help me? Was it possible that I could live without drinking? I sat there a long time, wavering between a rising hope and a hovering fear of defeat. Slowly, I reached out and picked up the phone.

It was dark the next evening when I pulled into the parking lot of the Council on Alcoholism. My appointment was for six o'clock. I turned off the engine and sat there, unable to move. I was afraid to get out of the car. What if they couldn't help me? What if this were just another blind alley. *But what else can I do?* I reasoned. *Maybe this is my only chance.*

I got out of the car and walked into the office.

A tall white-haired man with a friendly face was sitting at a desk in the small, sparsely furnished room. He smiled as he stood up to greet me.

"Hi. It's Pat, isn't it? I talked with you on the phone yesterday. Would you like some coffee?" I nodded, and he walked over to a table where a coffee pot was steaming.

"How did it go today?" he said casually, handing me a cup.

"Have you had a drink today?" His voice was comforting and I began to relax.

"I only drink at night, Mr. . . ."

"Call me Dudley. Not into the morning drink?" He smiled. "I could never face a day without a drink in the morning."

"Do you still drink every morning?" I asked.

He laughed. "No, those days are over. I haven't had a drink in twelve years." He smiled again.

"That's incredible," I said. "You see, I can't stop. And I can't fight it anymore. I drink every day now, and I can't stop." The words rushed out. It was such a relief to be able to talk about my shameful secret.

He nodded, and replied softly. "I know how it feels. But you don't have to drink." There was no arrogance in his words, just a quiet confidence.

"But I can't stop myself. I can't." I insisted. "I've tried and it's no use."

"The compulsion will pass," he said with quiet authority. "The need to drink will pass."

"But how?"

"One day at a time. Sometimes one hour at a time. You're in a good place, do you know that? You know *you* can't conquer it. That's the beginning of recovery.

"You see, Pat, alcoholism is an illness, a progressive illness. And it destroys. It kills—first the spiritual life, then the emotional life and, finally, the physical life. And recovery progresses in reverse order, first physical, then emotional and, at last, spiritual health." He smiled at me. "And that's the most important part of recovery, the recovery of your spiritual life."

"I don't know what a spiritual life is," I said flatly. "I don't have any faith."

"You will," he said firmly. "Just give it time."

"I don't know about that," I said with a sigh. "All I want is to stop drinking."

I could not think past the urge, which even that

moment, was beginning to gnaw at me again. But my protests did not deter my new friend. He began telling me about a meeting where people gave you support and encouragement with your struggles. And then he mentioned a woman named Joan who would be willing to meet me and go along to a meeting that very night. He reached for the phone.

Suddenly, I was aware that he was calling this Joan whoever she was—certainly a perfect stranger to me—and asking her to meet me. He was expecting me to step out of my closet and go to a meeting of unknown people who would take one look at me and know why I was there.

I wanted to interrupt him, to protest that I didn't want to meet anyone. There had to be another way. But I didn't say anything. I sat quietly and let him make the arrangements.

"All set, Pat." Dudley handed me a piece of paper with the address and time of the meeting. "Joan will meet you at the door. You just go and listen. You don't have to say anything or do anything. Just be there. There's nothing to be frightened about. You're not alone. Just remember, you don't ever have to drink again."

"That would take a miracle," I said grimly.

He smiled. "Miracles happen, Pat, You'll see."

I did meet Joan that night, nervous and wondering what I'd let myself in for. Joan was a pretty blonde in her mid-forties. She led me inside the church hall where the meeting was being held.

When I walked in, I was amazed at the sight. I half-expected to find the falling-down-drunk types, the unshaven, unwashed wretches that you see along the street. Perhaps I had built that mental image as a defense, because inside I thought I must surely be better than "the typical drunk." But by comparison with these happy, clear-eyed, and well-dressed men and women, I was a miserable mess.

The speaker that night, an army colonel, told about his thirty-year bout with alcoholism. Once again, as with the speaker I had heard at church the previous Sunday, the details of his story were foreign to me. But somehow I knew all about his feelings, knew firsthand the anguish he had lived through. It was my anguish he talked about.

As I drove home, the words of hope and encouragement blazed like a beacon in my mind, and I knew that I would not have to drink that night.

I went to more meetings that week—and the following week. And a miracle did happen: The compulsion to drink lifted. It simply stopped. The iron claw that had held me in its grip all of those tortured years lost its power over me. I dared to believe—to begin to believe—that I could recover.

Chapter Nine

Even as I made my first steps toward freedom from alcohol, I discovered that there would be no recovery for my marriage. Bert had moved from awareness of my problem, to frustration and finally to indifference. His stays in the city got longer and longer. As I had grown more self-involved—self-consumed—so had he. Alcoholism had struck at the heart of our marriage, killing every root of hope. And without hope nothing can live.

It was over quickly. I could hardly believe it. The divorce papers. The proceedings. The house on the lake had to be sold. The children and I moved to a smaller house, and Bert moved back to New York City. I was confronted with the task of facing life squarely for once. I had to learn to live in reality.

For two years I continued going to regular meetings. They had given me so much support and love, so much good, practical guidance, I knew I could not stay sober without them. I was filled with gratitude.

At a meeting one night in 1976, a speaker named Ron spoke eloquently about his uphill struggle in sobriety. He had lost his job, his house had burned down, and his marriage was breaking up. Yet, he spoke with humor, honesty and an utter lack of self pity that intrigued me.

"I get down on my knees every night," he told us, his dark eyes shining, "and thank the living God for my sobriety, and I ask his help to stay sober each day. I know he hears my prayer. He never fails me."

I was moved by his words and yet they disturbed me, the same disturbance I felt when others in the fellowship spoke about God and prayer. For two years, I had tried to sidestep all of the group's "God talk." Then, as the incredible triumph of being sober began to dim, I felt a restless dissatisfaction emerge within me. I didn't want to drink, but I wanted something—the something I saw shine in Ron's eyes and I heard in the voices of the people who knew how to pray. Where did they get this unquenchable faith?

After the meeting, I decided to ask Ron about it.

"I need to talk to someone about . . . faith, I guess you call it."

"What about faith?" he asked.

I blurted it out. "I don't have it, Ron. I listen to people like you who talk about praying to God as if . . . as if . . . you knew him personally."

He nodded thoughtfully. Then he said, "Let's go for a cup of coffee and talk about it."

At a local diner, we settled into a booth and I began to pour out my dilemma.

"I've tried to pray but I don't know who I'm praying to. At first, it didn't seem important, but now, I don't know, there's something I need, something I want. 'A Power greater than myself,' I think it's called." I laughed.

"I know about booze, that's a power greater than myself. For a long time I didn't want anything to do with all of the spiritual talk I've heard at the meetings. Well, I'm worried now. I understand that I have to turn my will and life over to God." I looked at his quiet, serious face. "But I don't know who God is."

"Ask Him," Ron responded simply.

I looked at him questioningly. He was quite serious.

"Ask Him? How do I do that?"

"By asking. Did you ever read the Bible?"

"Not really. Just for a literature course a few years ago."

"Read it," he said. "Read the gospel of Matthew, chapter seven. It's about asking, and receiving."

I was about to protest. He smiled again. "Just try it, Pat. Don't analyze it, just do it."

"Okay," I agreed. "I will. I'm learning at this late date to do what I'm told."

"Good," he replied. "Then we'll talk some more."

When I got home that night, after fixing supper for the children, I went to my bookshelf and looked for the Bible I had used in my college course. *I'll read it*, I thought, reaching up for the large volume. *It seems futile, but I'll do it.*

Taking the Bible into the bedroom, I set it on the table next to my bed. I stretched out, glad that the long day was over. I was very tired. My job was going well, but I felt as though I were living on a treadmill again. My life as a single parent was difficult. I lived with the constant awareness of my children's anger. Although they said nothing about it, their lack of response, their sometimes hostile attitudes, told me that they blamed me for the divorce. Silently, I accepted the blame. I didn't know what to do with the remorse and guilt that never left me. They continued to see their father on weekends, but I knew their lives had been damaged. I didn't know how to make it up to them.

I glanced at the Bible on my night table and picked it up. I found the gospel of Matthew and started to read, plowing through the genealogy of Christ, then the familiar story of His birth, the beatitudes, and the Lord's Prayer. The words were beautiful, but they held no meaning for me.

I may as well go to sleep, I thought. Then I remembered that Ron had told me to read the seventh chapter. I turned to the right page and began to read again: "Ask, and it shall be give you; seek, and you will find; knock, and it will be opened to you."

How wonderful, I thought, *if that were true. Just ask and seek and knock . . . but who do I ask?* I kept reading.

"What man of you, if his son asks him for bread, will give him a stone? Or if he asks for a fish, will give him a serpent? If you, then, who are evil, know how to give good gifts to your children, how much more will your father who is in heaven give good things to those who ask him?"

Fathers give good gifts . . . as I read the words over again I felt a deep rage stirring inside of me. What good gifts had my father given me? Those were fine words, but they didn't include me. What do you do if your father gives you a serpent? My anger seethed at the unseen God who had no answers for me.

I'm not one of the chosen ones, whose fathers love them and give them good gifts.

"What kind of God are you?" I surprised myself by speaking out loud. "You promise things that can't happen for people like me. I can't change the past, so what can I hope for? It's too late for me!" I threw the book down and turned out the light.

The 'Good Book,' I thought bitterly. *It's okay for Ron, but it isn't meant for me.*

Fathers give good gifts. . . . Those words kept repeating in my mind as I fell asleep. Through that restless night I swam up current once more, searching for a distant light that was always too far off to reach.

The next morning I put the Bible back on my night table. *I won't think about it anymore,* I decided. *I'm sober now, I have a fellowship I love, and that's a miracle enough for me.*

I went through my busy day completely absorbed in the tasks before me, determined to shut out any deep thoughts.

That night after the meeting Ron came over and sat beside me. "How's it going?" he asked.

I took a deep breath and let the words out. "I just don't believe. I try to pray, but I don't feel anything. Nothing happens."

He didn't argue with me. He listened thoughtfully and then said, "Let's take first things first," Ron said. "First, are you sober?"

"Yes! Sober two years now. You know that, Ron." What was he getting at?

"And did you get yourself sober?"

"No," I admitted readily. "I couldn't get myself sober."

"Then, who got you sober?"

"Well, the program did, of course."

"And where did the program come from? What did the founders say about it?"

I quoted the words I had to read so often: "There is One who has all power. May you find Him now." I slumped back in my seat. "I haven't found him, Ron. And I don't know how. It's different for you. You have faith. God is there for you."

He laughed softly. "Yes, He's there. He's always there. But I didn't know that for a long time." He leaned forward and looked at me intently. "Pat, faith isn't a feeling. Faith is an action."

"What do you mean, an action?"

His face was bright with the certainty of his words. "Sometimes faith is doing what you don't feel, what you don't understand. Praying is an act of faith, even when you don't know who you're praying to."

"Is that what you did?"

"Yes, lots of times. I prayed for a long time before I knew God was there for me. I prayed because I didn't know what else to try. So I decided to do what the people in the fellowship were telling me to do." He smiled reassuringly. "I prayed for a long time to God as I *didn't* understand Him."

"And now you understand him?" I asked, incredulous.

"Not by a long shot," he said. "But I know, if I'm willing, He'll answer me when I ask for His help."

"Ask and you shall receive," I quoted, mirthlessly. "I read that in the Bible last night."

"And what did you think about it?"

I didn't want to talk about my father and the feelings of rage the passage had stirred up in me. I gathered my thoughts. "Ron, if I'm going to pray, I can't pray into a void. If I'm going to make collect calls to the Almighty, I've got to know there's someone there to take them!"

We were silent a moment. Then Ron said, "Pat, can you ask God to reveal Himself to you, in your life, in a way that you can understand?"

"I guess I could do that," I said slowly. "Can you do that, even if you don't believe?"

"*Especially* if you don't believe," he answered.

"Try it, for two weeks, every night. And see what happens."

I looked at his calm, serious face. There was the certainty of God in his eyes. He had found something important, something I needed in my life.

"Okay, Ron. I'll do it," I said.

That night, alone in my room, feeling awkward and self-conscious, I began to pray. "God, whoever, wherever You are, I'm here to ask You to reveal Yourself to me in a way that I can understand. Ron says that You'll answer me. So I'm asking and I'm going to keep asking for two weeks. I need to know if You're real."

That's not much of a prayer, I thought. I searched my mind for something more to say. I waited a moment and then said, haltingly, "And thank You for getting me sober and thank You for keeping me sober today."

I had done what I was supposed to do and I could do no more. That night, I slept peacefully.

I continued my prayer commitment every night. As the days went by, I felt less self-conscious about it. Talking to God seemed to get easier.

"I think I'm getting the hang of it," I told Ron.

"How do you feel about it now?" he asked.

"Nothing's happened. But then, I don't really know what to expect. At first, I felt like a hypocrite, but I decided to say what I feel, without editing."

"Good," he said. "You can't keep any secrets from Him, anyway. Have you read any of the Psalms?"

"No, I haven't. I hadn't read the Bible at all since the troubling passage about fathers and serpents."

"The Psalms help me a lot." Ron offered. "David cries his heart out to God, lets it all hang out and then he's ready to give thanks and praise. God accepts it all. He knows us, Pat. Every hair on our heads is counted."

I thought about Ron's words after my prayer time that night. *He knows us.* That was comforting. I didn't know if it were true, but I hoped so. Slowly, I was beginning to realize how much I wanted to believe. Whatever it was that Ron and others in the fellowship had, I finally accepted that it was real.

As the two weeks progressed, I began to notice a change in myself. My anxiety diminished and I had a feeling of confidence that I could not explain. Outwardly, nothing was different, but something was happening within. I found I was looking forward to prayer time, and so I began to pray in the car as I drove home from work. The prayers were a silent conversation with an unknown presence. As I drove toward Route 7, I would pray: "I don't know if You're hearing me, but it makes me feel better talking to You, whoever You are." I would laugh out loud. "And I hope You have a sense of humor!"

On Friday night at the end of the second week, I left the office, tired from the hectic days I'd been through. I was looking forward to a weekend without pressure. Chris and Jennifer were going into the city to spend the weekend with Bert. It was a warm September evening and I was glad there was some daylight left as I headed out onto the highway. It was the same familiar route, the same familiar feeling of relief that at last it was Friday.

And then, with no warning, as I approached the Route 7 intersection, a heavy cloud of depression descended over me. Wave after wave of fear and loneliness engulfed me, pulling me down to an all too familiar despair.

Oh, God! What's happening? I've been feeling so good, I don't understand this. I slowed to a stop at the traffic light. My heart was racing.

"Oh, God, what's wrong with me?" I cried aloud.

Gripping the steering wheel, I stared straight ahead at the car in front of me, a red car with a Vermont license plate. For some reason, the white figures on the green plate drew my attention: *FX 309*.

And suddenly, there it was in my mind's eye, like an image projected on a movie screen: 309 Warwick Avenue, the tree-lined street, the sidewalk where I'd play hopscotch, the wooden seats on the front porch. And there was my father's black car in the driveway. My mind's eye opened the front door, and there stood Father. I hated him—and yet . . . And then I heard a voice, a presence in my mind I knew only I could hear . . . "Your father . . . you must fix your relationship with your father . . ."

I cried out. "He's gone! I don't even know if he's alive. I couldn't build a relationship with him even if I could find him!" A single word came to me: *Nevertheless*.

The red car with the Vermont plates turned off at an intersection and vanished.

I was almost home. The vision of Warwick Avenue passed, and my pounding heart slowed to a normal pace. My hands ached from clutching the steering wheel.

When I pulled into the driveway, I shut off the engine, and rested my head against the steering wheel. Then I began to speak to the One who had spoken to me. "I don't have to ask if that was You, God," I said. "I know it was. And I know what You've shown me is true." I felt the tears running down my face.

"I know what's wrong. I know I still hate my father. And I don't know what to do about it. Help me, oh God, help me!"

At the meeting that night, Ron came over and sat down next to me. He waited for me to speak. I turned to him and said, "You were right, Ron. God is alive and He answers prayers."

He smiled. I knew he understood. "He answered me today. And I don't like the answer."

"Why is that?" Ron asked quietly.

"Because I don't know how to do what He's asked of me."

"Then seek Him, Pat," he said simply. "Just keep on seeking."

At the close of the meeting we said the Lord's Prayer. The words held a new meaning. "Forgive us our trespasses as we forgive those who trespass against us."

Over coffee in the diner later, I told Ron the whole story. "I can't forgive my father," I protested. "I just don't have it in me."

Ron thought a moment, then asked, "Can you say the words?"

"Sure, I can say it," I answered, "But I can't mean it."

"Say it anyway," he told me. "Just say the words when you pray."

"What good will that do?"

"Ask God to help you make the words real," he answered. "Remember that faith isn't a feeling, it's an action. Do it as an act of faith."

I shook my head doubtfully, then agreed. "All right," I told him.

That night I began a new prayer vigil. "God, I haven't forgiven my father. I'll say the words now: I forgive my father. I'll keep saying them everyday. Help me to forgive, because I can't do it without You." The prayer felt leaden.

Even worse, I could picture my father's face, the

hard lines around his mouth, the cold, accusing eyes. Accusing me of what? He had betrayed *me.* He had left me. Why should I forgive him?

"It's impossible!" I cried. "I can't! Why do You ask me to do the impossible?"

Again the one-word reply came: *Nevertheless.*

"Then You'll have to do it. You have the power, so I give up."

At once, a surge of relief filled me, as if unseen hands had lifted all my anguish.

The following week I was asked to fly to Pittsburgh and spend the day working out some problems with a business presentation I was putting together. It was a long, hard day and I was glad when the session was over. I hated traveling alone, and I felt restless waiting around the airport for my flight home. With half an hour to kill before flight time, I strolled into a small shop, looking for something to read on the plane. I wandered around the store, glancing at paperbacks and souvenirs. Nothing appealed to me.

As I was leaving the store, I noticed a showcase near the door. Among a collection of bracelets and gold chains something caught my eye. Resting on a cushion of red velvet was a small gold cross with a pearl in the center. It was unobtrusive, ordinary really, but it held me to the spot. Impulsively, I knew I had to buy that cross. I didn't want to get on the plane without it.

This is absurd, I thought, I had rejected the Resurrection long before—Jesus, to me, was merely a good man, certainly not my savior.

I started to leave, then turned back and asked the clerk to show me the cross. She took it out of the case and I held it in my hand.

"Yes," I said firmly. "I'll take this."

"Shall I wrap it for you?"

"No," I answered, "I'll wear it."

I paid her, fastened the chain around my neck and tucked the cross inside my blouse.

Why am I doing this? I wondered, as I hurried to board the plane. *Am I getting superstitious?* I fastened my seat belt and as the plane lifted from the ground, I could feel the comforting touch of the metal cross resting against my skin.

I won't tell anyone about this, I thought. *I don't even have a right to wear it. I don't believe in Jesus Christ.*

I didn't understand it. It was irrational. But somehow I didn't feel so lonely as I looked out at the darkening skies.

Several weeks later, at a regular Thursday night meeting, I turned to Joan, who had become a close friend.

"What step are we doing tonight?" I asked, as we took our seats at the table. The "Step Meetings" were my favorites. Slowly, methodically, they were helping me to straighten out my life.

"Step nine," Joan answered. "Making amends to those we've harmed. That's going to take most of my life, I'm sure."

A pretty red-haired woman named Winnie led the meeting that night. With quiet assurance she told us briefly about her drinking years and her recovery.

"We can never be sure," she said, "that the amends we try to make will be accepted by those we have harmed. They have the right to reject us and sometimes they do. It's happened to me. Of course I felt disappointed, but I needed to try, for my own sake, to clean out the bitterness and resentment that lingered on long after the drinking was over."

In the discussion that followed, my mind kept riveting on my father. When it was my turn to speak,

I knew I had to share my feelings with the group. "My father . . . ," I faltered, then began again. "My father left us when I was a teenager, and I've never been able to forgive him."

"Do you see your father?" Winnie asked.

"No, I haven't seen him in sixteen years. I've prayed about this, but I don't see any way I can make amends now. It's too late."

"It's never too late," Winnie answered.

"But I don't even know if he's alive," I protested.

"If he's still living, how old would he be?" she asked.

"In his late seventies—about seventy-eight."

She replied, gently, "Then you may not have much time left, Pat."

Fear swept over me. Then anger. "What can I do? I don't know how to find him."

"Are there any relatives you could contact?" she asked.

"Yes," I said reluctantly. "I have a cousin in Albany. We exchange Christmas cards every year."

"Well, then," Winnie answered. "You have a place to start."

"But it's so difficult. After all," I argued, "He's the one who hurt us! If anyone has amends to make, it's him, not me."

"I know it's difficult," she answered. "But, nevertheless . . ."

Nevertheless. I didn't hear another word she said. I didn't have to.

"Why do I have to make the first move?" I demanded.

"Because you're sober, Pat. It's up to you."

I knew she was right. I couldn't deny the simple truth of her words.

"I'll have to think about it," I responded lamely.

"Don't wait too long, Pat," Winnie advised. "God is giving you a chance you may never have again."

Over the next two weeks I resolved every day to go to the phone and call my cousin. And every day I postponed it. "I'll do it tomorrow," I would promise; tomorrow was time enough. But the word kept coming back to me—*Nevertheless.*

One evening as I was finishing up the supper dishes, a friend from the group called me. John had been sober for over a year. His life was now centered in his relationship with God. He had always been brotherly and affectionate, someone I could talk openly with.

"We've talked a lot about turning our lives over to God," John said, "and I've been thinking over what you told us at the meeting the other night about your father."

"I haven't done anything about it," I said defensively. "I'm no closer to making that phone call than I was last week."

"Patty, I want to tell you about something that's helped me. For the past few weeks I've been going to a prayer meeting and it's made a tremendous difference in my life. I can pray now in a way I never could before. I think it could help you, too."

"I have barely gotten comfortable praying alone, John. I don't see myself praying in a group." The idea of people praying together seemed absurd to me.

"You don't have to pray out loud, Pat. It's very informal."

"Well, what do you do?"

"Sometimes we sing, sometimes we just sit quietly. Sometimes I just sit and listen to the others pray, while I pray silently. But something wonderful happens in that room. Why don't you come tomorrow night?"

"John, I'm not religious. I'm not really a Christian." I saw no point in hiding the truth.

"A year ago," he said, "I couldn't say the name Jesus—except as a curse. I didn't know what forgiveness meant. Now I know that in Christ I am forgiven and I can forgive others."

"I don't understand why you need a prayer meeting," I argued. "You have the fellowship, and it keeps you sober."

"The prayer meeting has answered a question for me, Pat," he explained. "In all the years I've gone to church, I never had the answer. Now I know Christ is God, as I understand Him."

"Thanks, John," I said wearily. "I appreciate the invitation, but it's not for me."

Later that night, I puzzled over John's words. What did Jesus Christ have to do with me?

As I reached over to turn off the bedside light, I noticed the little gold cross resting on my night table. I recalled that evening at the airport when I knew I had to have it. Again, I wondered why I'd bought it, and why I wore it every day beneath my blouse.

It was raining heavily when I left the office the following night. I had worked late and I felt tired to my very bones. Since it was Friday, the children would be with their father.

I glanced at the clock on the dashboard. It was ten of eight. *John must be at his prayer meeting now,* I thought. I was glad he found what he was looking for. *Seek, and you will find,* I thought.

Suddenly, I made a decision. Quickly I turned the car around and drove toward the church school where his group met.

It was a little past eight when I walked into the

auditorium. About fifty people were gathered in a circle in the center of the room. John looked up and waved to me as I found a seat.

Two young men were playing guitars and everyone was singing. It was a simple melody, resounding with "Hallelujah" and "Praise to the Lord." *What am I doing here?* I wondered, as the woman next to me handed me a songbook and pointed out the right page.

The song ended and a hush fell over the room. I settled back in my chair. At least it was restful. I could sit quietly for a little while.

Then people began to pray. A pretty, young, dark haired woman began to speak. "Thank you, Lord, for coming into my life. I praise you for giving me a new life. Thank you, Lord, for dying on the cross for me, for defeating death in your Resurrection. Thank you for making me a new creation."

Others poured out their prayers of thanksgiving. The prayers swelled to a crescendo and then receded to a peaceful silence. I felt the peace washing over me.

Then, a sound like bells echoing in the wind rose up from the group. They were singing without song books now, in an unfamiliar language. The melody wandered, lifted and fell, rose again, the voices blending in beautiful harmonies. My weary spirit lifted with the melody. The singing ended and the room was silent once again.

"Ask, and it will be given you; seek and you will find," someone was reading aloud the now familiar passage. "Knock, and it will be opened to you. For everyone who asks, receives and he who seeks finds and to him who knocks it will be opened." The words seemed less difficult to believe.

I sat quietly for a long time, savoring the new

peace that filled me, hardly conscious that the meeting had ended. The woman next to me touched my arm.

"Hello," she said. "I'm Ruth. Is this your first time here?" Immediately, I liked her gentle smile that crinkled the corners of her warm brown eyes. "Yes." I said. "It was lovely. I really am surprised. I didn't know what it would be like."

"The Lord restores us here," she said simply.

Yes, that's how I felt. Restored.

We spoke for a few moments, and I asked her about the unusual singing. Graciously, she explained that they had been "singing in the Spirit." Some called it "singing in tongues," she said.

John came bounding over just then, grinning from ear to ear. "I don't have to ask if you liked it. I can tell by your face."

"Yes, I liked it very much. I can't explain it, but I felt a deep peace tonight."

"That's from the Holy Spirit," he answered. "I've felt it, too. Are you coming next week?"

"Yes, I think I will," I answered.

That night, when I'd settled into bed, I opened the Bible and read again that passage in Matthew, chapter seven. The words, at last, filled me with comfort. I read the pamphlet Ruth had given me as I left. It said the Lord promised another Comforter, the Holy Spirit.

I got out of bed, knelt down and began to pray. "Lord, I know who You are now. Your name is Jesus. And I think I've been running away from You most of my life. But there's so much I don't understand. When I was a child, I believed in You. I know Christmas was real to me, Your birth was real. Even Your death on the cross, that was real to me."

I rested my head against the bed as I prayed. "But

Easter never came for me. They said You rose from the dead, and I've never felt that was true. Now You've given me a resurrection, a new life, but I can't handle it alone. It's too much for me. You said You would send another comforter, the Holy Spirit. I need the comforter, Lord, I need Him now. I'm giving You all of me, and I ask You to fill me up with Your everlasting love."

I rested at the side of my bed, still on my knees. I had prayed from the deepest part of my being. I felt emptied out, tired, but free of conflict. When at last I lay down to sleep, I felt a peace flowing through me, all of the fear and confusion washed away. I knew I would never have to hide that little gold cross again. I drifted into a deep sleep, knowing that the Spirit of God was truly with me that night.

The next morning I went to the phone to call my cousin in Albany. The time had come.

Martha was glad to hear from me. I stumbled through small talk until I couldn't prolong the important question any longer.

"Martha," I asked, my heart pounding in my ears, "have you had any news about my father?"

She seemed to sense that my question was important. "I haven't seen him in years, Patty. But I know Aunt Vera saw him about a year ago. She told me he had asked about you."

"Do you know where he's living?"

"I don't know his address, but I think he's living with his sister Tuti out on Long Island. Clara died—oh, it must be about eight years ago." She paused a moment. "Tell you what, Patty. Why don't you call Aunt Vera and get his address. I have her number."

The call to Aunt Vera brought the news that my

father was in a nursing home. I was beginning to sense that I was acting none too soon. Aunt Vera gave me the phone number of my father's sister, where he had indeed lived most recently.

That phone call was very difficult.

Aunt Tuti was about to move to Maine to live with her son, she explained, as she hunted up the number of the nursing home. There was nothing else she could do for her brother, she said heavily. "It's a little late to do much," she added with a touch of coldness. "After all, your father is dying."

Chapter Ten

I found it so hard to call Sunny Acres Nursing Home. It was only after my sleep had been haunted by a ringing telephone, that I finally picked up the phone and received a very friendly reception from the nursing supervisor, Mrs. Burns.

The news was bad. Behind Mrs. Burns' professionally cheerful words, I could tell that he was so ill he might not even know me. I hung up the phone that morning ready to drop the whole thing. What was the point in going to ask forgiveness of a man who was unconscious?

John would not hear of my backing out, however. He even took a day off work to make the drive to Long Island with me. As we drove along the highway, he was as brisk sounding as I was dour.

"What a beautiful day for the drive," he said as we crossed the border from Connecticut into New York. I knew he had sensed my nervousness.

"I don't think I could have done this alone," I responded, gratefully.

John turned and smiled at me. "Patty, we're not alone."

"But what am I going to accomplish by this? He won't even know me," I said.

"You just get there," John replied. "Everything else is in the Lord's hands."

A comforting peace surrounded me during the long drive. That is, until we turned into the entrance of the nursing home. As we came to stop in front of the pleasant brick building, I knew I could not do it. I wanted to run, as I had always run. I sat motionless.

"What's the matter, Patty?" John asked.

"I'm afraid. I'm afraid of seeing him. Afraid he might reject me one more time. I don't know what I'll do if . . ." The words caught in my throat. Suddenly I felt the weight of the enormous risk I was taking emotionally.

John took my hand. "This journey is in the Lord's will for you. Let's just trust Him."

Inside a tall, gray-haired woman in a crisp white uniform was sitting at the nurses' station.

She stood up and extended her hand. "I'm Mrs. Burns. I'm so glad you've come. Your father is going back to the hospital today, and I was hoping you'd be here in time."

"How is he?" I asked.

"He's slipping away, mostly unconscious. We have him sitting up for brief periods, but there's no communication. He can't speak and he doesn't seem to hear. He hasn't eaten anything in three days."

"Can I see him?"

"Oh, yes," she said, and took my arm. "I just wanted you to be prepared. I'll take you to him."

She led us down the corridor to his room. At the door I stopped, frozen in my tracks. I couldn't believe what I saw. There, wrapped in a gray bathrobe, was a frail, old man, propped up in a wheelchair. His body was shaking with tremors and he groaned feebly. I sat down next to him and picked up one cold, trembling hand.

"Hello, Daddy." My voice choked.

I looked over at John. He nodded encouragingly.

Then I looked at the vacant staring eyes, the thin mouth hanging slack and listened to the whimpering sounds coming from the palsied body of the man who was my father. His mind seemed lost, wandering in darkness. There was no sign of recognition.

"Talk to him, Patty, just talk to him," John said softly. "I'll be waiting outside."

I sat there alone with my father, holding his hand. In a few minutes, I tried to speak.

"Daddy, it's Pat. I'm here." He groaned and his shoulders shook. I went on stroking his limp hand, searching for strength to say the next words.

"Daddy—Daddy, I love you." As the words came out, something happened, as real as if a warm current had suddenly washed into the room, melting the cold, hard knot that had bound my heart for so many years.

In that moment, pain was gone, and fear.

"I love you, Daddy." It felt so good, through the tears of joy, to say these words. "I'm sorry that I hurt you so much. And I forgive you for everything that's happened."

He moaned a little. I had no idea whether my words had reached him inside where he was wandering in his private darkness. His glassy eyes kept staring ahead. Tears were rolling from my eyes—not tears of anger or bitterness, but tears of cleansing.

I stayed there with him a long time, hardly conscious of time passing. I talked to him some more, not caring whether he could hear me or not. Occasionally, he interrupted my words with a groan.

Eventually, I knew it was time to go. John had been waiting for me. "I'm going to be leaving you now, Daddy." It had taken so long for us to find each other that now I could hardly say good-by. And this was really good-by, probably the final one, since Mrs. Burns had said they were about to transfer him to the hospital. The expected him to die any day, perhaps any hour.

As I stood to leave, I squeezed his thin hand. And suddenly, I knew there was something else I had to do. Slowly, with a good deal of self-consciousness, I walked behind his chair and rested my hands on his trembling shoulder.

"Oh, Lord," I prayed aloud, "I ask You to bless my father. Fill him with Your peace. Let him know that You love him and that I love him, too." The last part was very hard to get out. "Lord, release him from this suffering. We've all suffered enough."

I leaned over and kissed Father's cold forehead. Then I hurried from the room.

"I'm ready to go now," I said when I found John at the nurses station. Turning to Mrs. Burns, I said, "Thank you for taking such good care of him."

She smiled warmly and squeezed my hand. "God bless you, dear. I'll call you and let you know."

As we drove away from the home, John turned to me and asked, "How do you feel now?"

"I'm glad I went," I said. "I wish I'd gotten there sooner, but I don't hate him now, and I'm not afraid of him. I'm just so sorry. Sorry it took so long.

"In the Lord's time, Patty," he answered softly. "Everything is in the Lord's time."

Chapter Eleven

One Sunday morning, two weeks later, the phone rang, waking me from a sound sleep.

"I have a collect call from Sunny Acres Nursing Home for Mrs. Zimmerman. Will you accept?"

I was wide awake now. "Yes, operator, I'll take the call." *Here it is,* I thought. I knew the call had to come eventually. I braced myself and waited for Mrs. Burns to come on the line and tell me my father was gone.

"Hold one moment please. Here is your party." I waited. Then a familiar voice said, "Hello, Patty?" But it was a man's voice.

Catching my breath, I said, "Who is this?"

"This is your father, Patty."

"Daddy!" I shouted into the phone. "Is that really you?" *I'm still asleep,* I thought, and *I'm having a very strange dream.*

"It's me, all right." The voice was a bit shaky, but it was my father's voice.

"Daddy, what's happening?" I didn't know what to say.

"I want to get out of this place," he declared. "I don't know what's the matter around here. They can't find my sister. I need my clothes, Patty, and I need to get in touch with Jim so he can pick me up. Now, I want you to call Jim for me, and tell him—"

"Wait a moment, Daddy," I interrupted, then laughed. Yes, that was my father all right, giving orders.

"Put Mrs. Burns on the phone for a moment, Daddy I need to talk with her."

"Hello, dear." It was Mrs. Burns, her voice unusually warm.

"Mrs. Burns, what's happened?"

She laughed heartily. "We don't know. He went to the hospital as near death as he could be, and came back eight days later with all of his faculties intact!" She laughed again. "He's walking up and down the corridors now, telling everyone he's got to get out of here—and he's got a chess tournament going on in the day room."

"It's incredible!" I gasped.

"Yes, dear, it's just that! The patients here cluster around him. They call him Lazarus."

"Mrs. Burns, this is impossible. I never dreamed—"

"Neither did we," she assured me. "He's been blessed with a miracle."

"What does he need, now?" I was eager to help in any way I could. "Can he really leave the nursing home?"

"Yes, the doctors say he's ready to go. I'll put him back on the phone now. He's getting impatient to tell you himself."

My father's first instructions were to find his sister. "Do you have Tuti's phone number, Patty? I don't know where she's gone."

"She's gone to Maine, Daddy, to stay with Tommy. I'll reach her for you and call you back in a little while."

"Well, someone has to pick me up here," he insisted. "I don't have my car. And then I'll need my clothes—"

"Everything will be taken care of, Daddy. Don't worry."

When I gave my aunt the incredible news, she couldn't believe it. "It's true, Tuti," I assured her. "He's in rare form." She promised to call him right away.

As I hung up the phone Chris came into my room. He gave me a puzzled look. I suddenly realized that he was seventeen years old and he knew nothing about his grandfather.

"Hey, Mom, what's all the commotion about? Who was that on the phone?"

"It was my father, Chris," I said.

He stared at me bewildered. "But I thought . . . didn't they tell you that he was . . ."

I was laughing and crying at the same time. "My father has come back from the dead! I don't know what happened, but he's alive and well!"

Chris grinned at me. His eyes lit up with excitement. "I've got to go tell Jen!"

He ran upstairs shouting the news to Jennifer.

I planned to go out to the nursing home and called my father to arrange the time. I was further surprised to learn that he had already reordered his life.

"I want to see you, Patty. Can you come to Maine?" His voice was strong and confident. "My friend Jim is driving me up to Tuti's on Sunday."

"So soon?" I asked. "Are you going to live there?"

"Yes, Tommy found an apartment for Tuti and me that's right in town."

I was happy for him, but Maine was so far away.

"Are you sure you're strong enough?" I asked. "After all, you're just getting back on your feet again." I was sure it was too soon for all these plans.

"I feel fine, Patty, and I'll feel even better when I get out of this mausoleum. And Tommy says there's great fishing up there, trout streams and lakes full of bass. . . ."

No, it wasn't too soon. I could hear it in his voice. He was ready to start living again.

"Okay, then," he said," I'll write as soon as I get up there and send you my address."

I had a moment of panic, remembering the times long ago when I waited for a letter that never came. There was nothing I could do—but trust.

Two weeks later, a letter arrived from Maine in my father's strong, firm handwriting. He gave a detailed chronology of his journey north and his enthusiastic reactions to his new home. I knew he was happy.

The following month, after Chris left for his first year in college, Jennifer and I drove to Maine at Father's insistence.

He greeted us at the door of the old colonial house where he and Tuti rented a spacious four room apartment. He stood tall and straight, thinner than I had ever known him to be. His face was lined, but had a healthy tan. He put his arms around me, and with a broad smile he said, "Well, you made it! Come on in. Dinner's just about ready."

I was overjoyed to see that my father's recovery was so complete. He was fully alert and full of energy and plans for the future.

The next day he drove us on a tour of the lovely little town he was so pleased to call home. He loved the cold, crisp air and the wide expanse of hills and waterways that surrounded him. He talked constantly about a special fishing trip coming up in the spring.

Before we left, I asked him if he remembered my visit to the nursing home.

"No, I don't remember anything that happened until I came back to the living in the hospital." He looked at me a long time, and then smiled. "The doctors don't know what happened. But I do. It was something about your visit that turned everything around."

"A lot of prayer, Daddy, a lot of people praying for you," I said. "That's what turned everything around."

"Maybe so, Patty," he smiled. "That's good enough for me. I don't know the answer, but I'm grateful to be here, grateful for whatever it was that happened."

Not exactly a proclamation of faith, I thought, *but, oh, what a long way my scornful, skeptical father had come.*

As Jennifer and I drove back to Connecticut, I thought about the long, hard journey through the pain-filled years that had brought me to this weekend visit in a little Maine village. I had come full circle; I had completed a healing journey I had never dreamed was possible.

The following April, a large fat envelope arrived from Maine. In it was a five-page letter from my father. I settled down on my living room sofa to read his meticulous account of his fabulous fishing trip on the Narragausus River—"one of the best salmon runs in the state," he wrote.

"I snagged nine out of the fourteen salmon we caught in two days. And on April 14, my eightieth birthday, I hit the jackpot." He was explaining something about a photograph. I shook the envelope. A photo fell out in my lap.

I continued reading Father's letter. "I had the guide take this photo just for you, Patty." He said the special catch was my prize, too. "The granddaddy of them all—over forty inches! Somebody up there must like me."

I stared at the picture he had sent: In it was my father, a broad grin on his lined face, the mountains and lake behind him—holding out to me an enormous, glistening salmon.

As I looked at the marvelous photograph, I wondered again at the miracle of my father's recovery, how complete it was. I had prayed that day in the nursing home that he wouldn't suffer, and now look at him! So alive, and loving every moment. And he was sharing it with me.

As I put the letter down on top of my Bible, which was resting on the coffee table, a sudden, startling thought raced through my mind. Quickly I opened the Bible and turned to the Gospel of Matthew, chapter seven. As my eyes scanned the words, I felt a rush of warm tears well up inside of me. My heart filled with an unspeakable joy.

"Oh, Lord!" I prayed through tears of joy. "After all these years! After all the times I've said my father gave me a serpent. Now in my hands, here is my fish."

Slowly I read aloud the words that I hadn't believed, the words that had taunted me:

"Ask, and it will be given you; seek, and you will find; knock, and the door will be opened to you. For every one who asks receives, and he who seeks finds, and to him who knocks it will be opened. Or what man of you, if his son asks him for bread, will give him a stone? Or if he asks for a fish, will give him a serpent? If you then, who are evil, know how to give good gifts to your children, how much more will your Father who is in heaven give good things to those who ask him!"

At last my lifelong dream had been fulfilled. I had longed for a different fish as a child, of course, the chance to win my father's approval and to make him proud of me. This fish came as a different symbol—a symbol of the power of unconditional love and forgiveness. It was Christ's forgiveness that had melted my own icy heart and brought to life a dying man. My heart filled with gratitude.

"Thank You, Jesus," I whispered. "Thank You for my fish."